VANISHED

Vanished

THE MARK DENNIS STORY

Steve Wilcox

Steven Wilcox

To Jerry
Rest in peace, my friend,
Our work is done.

On a hot day in July 1966, a CH-46 Sea Knight helicopter approached Landing Zone (LZ) Crow at Quang Tri Provence, South Vietnam. It was the sixth such helicopter to approach with combat Marine reinforcements on board. The first four approached from the west without incident. Then, however, winds changed, and the next four helicopters had to come from the south, flying over the dense foliage of the jungle.

A few minutes out, the lead helicopter began taking on enemy fine and ordered the mission aborted. Three of the four helicopters managed to evade enemy fire and escaped unharmed. The second, however, was hit before it could do the abort maneuver. With fire and smoke billowing out the aircraft's rear, the helicopter overshot the LZ, finally coming to rest on the side of a hill where it rolled over onto its starboard side. Only three crew members survived.

On this hot July evening, HM3 Mark V. Dennis, USN/FMF, simply vanished from the face of the earth. The Navy recovered what they believed were the remains of everyone on that helicopter except for Dennis. Unfortunately, all of the remains were burned too severely for visual identification. The morgue used dog tags to identify the bodies. Most were also able to be identified by dental charts.

All except Mark Dennis. No one found his dog tags. Nor was his aid kit found. There were no unidentified bodies from the events of that day. Where did he go? How could this tall, skinny kid from Miamisburg, Ohio, merely disappear?

Mark was my friend. From our days together at the Naval Hospital, Marine Corps Base, Camp Lejeune, North Carolina, he was my best friend. The barracks housed eight open cubicles, four on either side of a central walkway. Entering the barracks, he was the first cubicle on the right; I was the first one on the left. We hung out together, did extra duty together, and he introduced me to a student nurse I've been married to for more than fifty years.

In 1990, I became good friends with Mark's brother, Jerry, as Jerry decided to take Mark's story national in the hope of finding answers. He invited me to participate in the production of the *Unsolved Mysteries* "Missing Medic" episode. At the end of the show, there was a toll-free number to call with any information. More than 400 calls were received that night, a record for any episode thus far. Unfortunately, none of the tips panned out.

With nothing left to pursue, the story died down, and I lost touch with Jerry. However, the *Lifetime Television Network*, a cable channel, would repeat the story for several years.

In 2014, I learned the Dennis family, through Mark's nephew, Bryan, had raised funds to test the DNA of the remains given to the family in 1966. Unfortunately, the remains were not related to the Dennis family. The government didn't budge, and the family eventually buried the cremated bones in the family grave alongside Mark's mother and father.

In June 2021, I decided to tell Mark's story. Mark's immediate family were all deceased, but he had an extended family and friends. So I decided to tell Mark's story in hopes of providing some closure to those of us who knew and loved this quiet young man.

Nothing prepared me for what I found. But then, just as I was beginning to put Mark's story together, I found him. There was a single paragraph on a United States Government website the remains of HM3 Mark V. Dennis USN/FMF were found and positively identified by DNA analysis. But, unfortunately, I discovered his family was unaware of this site or the information it contained.

Knowing where Mark had been all these years allowed me to resolve many of the questions Jerry raised in 1990 when we did the television show and questions his family and friends have had over the years.

Only three questions remain, and I doubt anyone can answer them with any certainty. First, the identity of the body the government gave to the Dennis family. Who was he? Based on what I now know, he was not at Quang Tri on that fateful day in July 1966. Second, why has it been so crucial Mark Dennis be identified? Why could not the government simply mark him *Missing in Action*? Finally, why the need for subterfuge? Despite the continual insistence, the remains given to the family were those of Mark; the government officially declared him MIA in 1990. When Mark was found in 2014 and positively identified, the government never informed the family of this momentous event. The cremated remains returned to the family with a DNA sample were, in fact, those of their family member. His sisters, Anne, and Eileen buried the cremated bones without knowing they were burying their brother.

The most satisfying aspect of this story, I have been able to fill in the gaps missing for fifty-one years, from the helicopter crash in 1966 to the burial of the bones in 2017. Hopefully, I have been able to provide a sense of closure for Mark's family and friends.

DT2 Steven E. Wilcox
(1964-1968)

October 2021

ACKNOWLEDGMENTS

This book could not have been possible without the help and support of the following individuals.

- My wife of 53 years has given me encouragement and support to write this book.
- Linda Williams, my wife's roommate in nursing school, is also her best friend and Mark's fiancée.
- Bryan Curtis, Mark's nephew, and a current family spokesperson, provided invaluable information and encouragement.
- Elsie Johnson, Mark's sister-in-law, provided support and fact-checking.
- Linda Erwin, Mark's cousin, read what I wrote and fact-checked along the way.
- Joe Rizzo – a former side gunner on a Sea Knight, provided a unique insight on the airship.
- James Swanson – a veteran, shared infinite wisdom and his ability to find hidden facts.
- Michael Waller – provided me with invaluable wartime information to keep me honest.
- Ironmen Bible Study – veterans provided insight, information, and encouragement.
- Becky Seale – my editor to ensure the book is readable
- Jerry Dennis – May he rest in peace, as he planted the seed some 31 years ago. I hope you are happy with what I have written and the answers I have found.

CHAPTER 1
Mark V. Dennis

In the 1940s, Piqua, Ohio, was a tiny farming community 30 miles north of Dayton. It was there on Monday, September 22, 1946, Charles and Vera Dennis welcomed their second son into the world. They christened him Mark V. Dennis. Mark would develop a signature response to the questions, "What does the V stand for?"

"V does not stand for anything; I do not have a middle name. It is not even a letter; the V is the Roman Numeral for the number 5. I am the fifth child. The period means finality. My parents decided I would be the last child."

While Mark was the fifth child born to Vera and Charles, he only knew three siblings. The fourth sibling, the second daughter, died shortly after birth, years before Mark was born.

Charles worked for the railroad and moved around. A few years in Piqua, the Dennis family found themselves forty miles northwest in the little town of St. Mary's. St. Mary's is on the southern coast of Grand Lake St. Mary's. Almost every artificial lake is formed by damming up a river. In the 30s, the Civilian Conservation Corps contracted men to dig, by hand, the lake where the marshland was.

Celina is a small town on the north shore of Grand Lake St. Mary's, and Charles spent a year or two at that station before being reassigned to the larger community of St. Mary's.

The family's stay in St. Mary's was short-lived and then transferred to the thriving metropolis of Dayton. The family settled in a small community just south of Dayton called Miamisburg. This community would be Mark's home through most of his school days, and it was his home when he enlisted in the Navy.

Mark was tall, quiet, and good-looking. During his senior year, he played tackle for the Miamisburg High School Vikings. According to the program, Mark stood 5-10 and weighed in at 156 pounds. Family members would recall Mark stood between 5-11 and 6-foot at graduation.

Mark was a deeply religious individual and was active in the Miamisburg Church of Christ. By the mid-sixties, profanity was making its way into pop culture, but Mark never succumbed to the temptation. When a situation arose where some might say hell or damn, Mark said his trademark curse word substitute, "Bullhonk." I asked him about it after hearing him say it a few times, and he said, "It is inoffensive, doesn't violate the teachings of the Bible, and it allows me to relieve my frustration or moment of anger."

Linda Mullins also attended the Miamisburg Church of Christ. Linda was in her first year of nursing school at the Miami Valley Hospital School of Nursing. When talking with her about those early days, she said she knew Mark and sort of liked him, but she did not think there was anything special. Mark, on the other hand, obviously had other ideas.

The Navy had a particular enlistment program where recruits would be guaranteed a school but would have up to six months after enlisting to report to Bootcamp. So, on February 4, 1964, Mark V. Dennis enlisted in the Navy. Unfortunately, for the first time, and unfortunately not the last, Mark would be the victim of some sloppy paperwork.

Enlisting in the Navy is not a particularly fun experience. Everyone is yelling at you, telling you where to go and where to stand. When standing, you pretty much stood at attention. There was a walkway with curtain cubicles on the left and people recording information on the right for your physical. Unfortunately, the Navy entered the essential information ahead of time, and the clerk is recording such mundane statistics as height, weight, eye color, and hair color. While Mark was not the tallest in his family, neither he nor his siblings were not short. We will never know how it happened, but someone recorded this six-foot, blue-eyed teenager as 5-7 ¼" tall with brown eyes. This error would prove both problematic and costly for Mark's family down the road.

My enlistment experience was a little different. I literally ran away from home to join the Navy. I snuck into my house to get my birth certificate and then snuck back and returned it. It was the only birth certificate I ever had, but it was not a legal birth certificate. By legal, I mean it was a ceremonial certificate issued by the hospital, but not the one on file with Los Angeles County. In addition, the induction center told me my birth certificate had a date of birth different than the one recorded by the county. The one in charge told me to call home and verify the date.

"I can't call home," I said to myself. "My parents don't know where I am!"

I did as was told. I went to the payphone, pretended to put a quarter in the slot, and dialed my home phone. I pretended to talk and reported back that my mother had verified my date of birth. Three or four days later, when I had to fill out some additional paperwork, I learned the Navy accepted my date of birth. But, for three or four days, I questioned the date of birth I had celebrated for 18 years!

If you were standing at attention and opened your folder, someone in uniform would come and get in your face and remind you of how much of a lowlife you were. It did not happen to me, but I did witness it. I never looked at the paperwork to see what date of birth the Navy had for me.

Likewise, Mark never looked at the information on his enlistment physical. He never knew there was an error in his height and eye color. Because he was unaware of it, he never corrected the information.

We both finished our induction ceremonies and took the oath, making us members of the United States Navy. After that, Mark went home to finish high school. Then, he would report to boot camp at the Great Lakes Training Center in July. A few weeks later, in August, I enlisted and boarded the bus to ride from Los Angeles to San Diego, where I did my Bootcamp.

Five weeks into Bootcamp, you are required to name your Military Occupation Specialty or MOS. There was a big, blue book with hundreds of job descriptions. I was interested in radio and television and saw "Training Devices Technician," and decided that was the job for me. The MOS was abbreviated TraDevMan, and when asked what I wanted to do in the Navy, I said, "I want to be a Tradevman."

"Corpsman or Dental Tech.?" the sailor asked.

"I really would like TraDevMan. It sounds really neat."

"Corpsman or Dental Tech?" he asked again.

"But." I started.

"Look, idiot. You can be a Hospital Corpsman and give shots all day or be a Dental Technician and work in an office and clean teeth. Those are your only options." He sat there staring at the paper, and he never looked up.

"Dental Technician," and I was off to learn to clean teeth.

Five weeks into his Bootcamp experience, Mark had the same decision to make. According to his brother Jerry, Mark considered being a missionary when he got out of the Navy, but Linda said he was considering becoming a pediatrician. Either way, given the same two options, he made the logical choice.

"Hospital Corpsman," he said.

There is a short break, leave as it is called in the military, for Mark between finishing basic training and heading to Hospital Corpsman School. He took that opportunity to go home and attend church with his family.

Linda recalls Mark arrived with Herbert Wollard and other friends. Herb was Mark's best friend, and they began making room for him. Mark spotted Linda and chose not to sit with his friends; he walked down the aisle to where Linda was sitting and asked if he could sit with her.

Linda said, "Of course," and made room for him. Mark was in his dress blue uniform. The uniform is made of dark blue wool, hence the term "navy blue," accented with white piping. Mark would have had two white stripes angling from upper right to lower left. The silk tie is rolled. We often used a dime to start the roll and tied it with a square knot, each side equal as they hung down from the knot. It was the first time Linda had seen Mark in uniform and immediately realized how handsome and how special Mark was.

In her words, "That's when I became smitten."

Linda's Sunday school group and others began writing service members in the Navy. Mark was writing to Linda, among others. After meeting Linda, he began to let the others know that he had started dating. From then on, his attention was on Linda.

Mark would go home as often as he could, Mark would go home to see his family and girlfriend. It was relatively easy while stationed at Great Lakes for Hospital Corpsman School, but Mark would make the trip whenever he could while stationed at Camp Lejeune up until that last leave before being deployed to Viet Nam.

Mark was a kind-hearted, soft-spoken young man. Elsie was a childhood friend with whom he would play Monopoly. Although only three months older, he was a year ahead of her in school. Elsie's brother married Mark's sister, Anne. Through Anne, Mark discovered Elsie had been invited to the prom and picked out a dress, and it was in lay-away. She was having difficulty making the final payment. Mark gave Elsie the money to retrieve her dress and make it to the prom.

I had the opportunity to meet Elsie as I researched this book, and there was a softness and kindness in her voice when she talked about Mark. Elsie, too, has a son named Mark in honor of her brother-in-law. She and Linda, Mark's fiancée, are good friends today, and Linda arranged the meeting. I think Mark would be tickled but a little embarrassed to find how many lives he touched and continues to influence today.

CHAPTER 2
Camp Lejeune

The Naval Hospital at the Marine Corps Base, Camp Lejeune, North Carolina, is located on a peninsula identified as Hospital Point. It is the only portion of the base guarded by the Navy Shore Patrol and not the Marine Military Police. It is also the only place on the base where sailors outnumbered marines. There was a white, two-story building just inside the gate that housed the unmarried WAVES. Driving up the road on the right were two red brick buildings. The first was the BOQ or Bachelor Officer's Quarters. A little further up was the OB/GYN building. Pregnant women were rarely allowed in the hospital proper and handled everything related to labor and delivery at this independent facility. It was the only medical department I did not work in while at Lejeune.

The hospital is a three-story, red-brick building with two wings off a central rotunda. There is a circular drive with six tall, wooden doors leading into the hospital. As you enter, the main desk is to the right, where everyone has to check-in. Behind the main desk area was the emergency room. Straight back is the cafeteria, and offices were to the left. An elevator was on the left at the entrance to the cafeteria hall. Wards and clinics were on the second floor, with the operating room suite and lab were on the third floor.

The hospital was an antique, even by 1960 standards. Phone calls came into the PBX switchboard, where a live person would plug a cord into the incoming hole on the switchboard and then put the connecting cable into the hole for the extension desired and push a toggle switch to make the phone ring. The paging system was a lighted sign with numbers 0-9. The pagers were located throughout the hospital. Doctors and selected staff had a page number. A bell or chime would sound, and the sign would light up with the number of the person being paged. That person would call the operator, who would connect them with whoever needed to talk to them.

I was at Camp Lejeune from May 10, 1965, through May 15, 1967. I always tell people, "I was at Camp Lejeune for two years and five days, which is two years and three days too long. It is a beautiful base, but you can see it all in two days."

My assignment was the oral surgery clinic. We did have a general dentistry room, and the junior doctor would handle those duties. We only saw those assigned to the hospital and hospital patients with dental emergencies. There were other dental clinics on the base for the Marine population. At least once a week, generally on Fridays, we were in the operating room repairing facial fractures from accidents and fights. There were a lot of accidents and fights!

My second and third week at Lejeune was in the operating room suite. There I learned the ins and outs of the surgical suite, from sanitizing the room after a procedure to circulating getting needed supplies to scrubbing and assisting the doctor in surgery. My first day on the job was a radical mastectomy, and they handed me the removed breast to take to the lab. I blushed, and everyone laughed. On my last day in the general surgery orientation, I assisted in the repair of three hernias.

Once every four or five weeks, I would have night duty, and my first night duty shift came the week after my surgical rotation. Night duty is a 12-hour shift from 6 pm to 6 am. My duties were at the front desk, where I would send out teletypes, work the switchboard, lower, and raise the flag, and whatever else was needed. It was during this night duty rotation that Mark Dennis and I crossed paths. While you had to go through the switchboard to make an off-base or outside call, you could dial directly to a station if you knew the extension. One evening, the desk phone rang.

"Hello," the OD or officer of the day said after picking up the phone. He gave me a quizzical look and said, "It's for you."

"Hello. This is Wilcox," I said into the phone.

"When you gonna come and get your junk off my bed?"

"Who is this?" I asked.

"Dennis. I've been assigned to this cubicle, but your junk is all over the bed. When are you going to move it?"

I explained the situation to the OD, who gave me 15 minutes to get everything cleared up. When I got to the barracks, Mark was waiting for me.

"Sorry about this," I said. Pointing to the cubicle across from where we were standing, "Robert Baker was discharged today. He said he would be gone by noon. He wasn't. He did not leave until after I had to report for the night shift."

"Not a problem," Mark said with a smile on his face. "I'm tired and want to get some sleep."

I finished moving "my junk," as Mark called it, out of my old cubicle and put in on the bunk in my new cubicle, and went back to work. We talked for a few more minutes and then went back to night duty.

I did not see Mark when he went to breakfast in the morning, and I was done with my night duty when he reported to the front desk getting directions to personnel. Not that anything had been planned, but we missed each other at lunch as well. He rolled in around four that afternoon. Although the chow hall opened at four-thirty for the evening meal, it was closed as he went by on the way to the barracks. My shift at the front desk did not start until six, so we headed off for dinner at five.

Over the next few weeks, Mark and I became good friends. On the weekend, Mark would learn of an auto accident or some other incident that overwhelmed the Intensive Care Unit or another floor.

"C'mon Wilcox, you haven't got anything better to do," Mark would announce, and we would head off to the hospital and volunteer our Saturday and/or Sunday afternoon. I learned a lot from Mark during this time. None of my training prepared me for working on the ward. I think that is where I developed my "never say no" attitude.

Through Mark, I got to know many regular corpsmen, and they saw I was not afraid to work. Eventually, I became a regular in the emergency room on the weekends. Regardless of who was on duty, the ER tech called me when a case came rolling into the emergency room, possibly requiring an oral surgeon. Not by the doctor, but whatever corpsman was on duty at the time.

Mark was impressed to learn I did a two-week rotation in general surgery. His notion of a dental tech was assisting the dentist with general dentistry procedures: filling cavities, pulling teeth, and cleaning teeth. He did not know about the oral surgery part of the MOS. I did not tell him I didn't either until I arrived. I got to impress him when I assisted with a bone graph. A marine came in with a cyst in his mandible or lower jaw. The cyst had grown so large that his jaw was paper-thin and susceptible to breaking. I assisted Dr. Kelly, our oral surgeon, in removing the cyst while an orthopedic surgeon removed a small portion of the marine's hip bone. I then assisted as Dr. Kelly put the bone fragment in place and wired the mouth shut.

Mark and I would splurge and go into town for a burger and a shake. Jacksonville, NC, was seven miles from the base, and most of us walked it. We were too cheap or too poor to pay for the cab ride into town and too impatient to wait for the bus that ran every thirty minutes. It was not a bad walk and, Mark and I would joke and talk about different things. He concluded my brain didn't work right when I shared how I set out for Beaufort, N.C., to visit a Bootcamp/dental tech school buddy.

"Look. My friend said it was a hop, skip, and a jump. I did not have a car at home and walked everywhere. So a 15–20-mile walk was nothing."

"And how far was your walk?" he asked, grinning.

"73 miles. One way, but I hitch-hiked part of the way."

Mark shook his head, looked down at the floor, and said, "Idiot!"

On Saturday, Mark invited me to join him in town. "I want to get Linda a pearl ring. Want to come and help me pick it out?"

After breakfast, we boarded the military bus to the front gate. As luck would have it, the city bus was there, and we rode it into town. We hit every jewelry store in the city, which meant about a dozen. Unfortunately, three retired marines owned most of the businesses in town, and so after about the third or fourth jewelry store, we started seeing the same merchandise over and over, but each store had a different price.

After a couple of hours, we gave up. The city bus had just arrived from the base, and it would be another thirty minutes before it would make a return trip.

"Let's walk," he said, and we set off for the base. Mark was returning disheartened and empty-handed. Me? Well, I spotted a $10 record player in a pawn shop.

"Nice purchase," Mark said. "Too bad you don't have any records."

"Not yet," I said, "but I am ready to find some records and listen to music."

It was July 3, and Mark had been at Lejeune for about five weeks. It was my birthday, and we had two desserts that night to celebrate. When we got back, he stopped me at the entrance to the dorm.

"Wilcox, you got a girlfriend back home?" he wanted to know.

"No," I answered, examining a new Roger Miller record I had just purchased.

"What about a girl. Writing a girl back home?" he persisted.

"No, I don't have a girlfriend back home, and I am not writing anyone. Why?"

"Want to write a nurse?" he asked with a broad grin on his face.

He explained his girlfriend, Linda, was a student nurse and had a roommate who wanted to write someone in the Navy. He gave me her name and address.

It took a few days to compose the letter. I did not want to sound like a lunatic. So I had Mark read it for his stamp of approval, and on July 7, I mailed Linda's roommate the letter.

A week later, I checked the mail in my mailbox, and there was this envelope. It was addressed to me with a Dayton, Ohio postmark. The return address showed it was from Judy Hollman, the student nurse!

Mark was working 3-11, and so I met him for mid-rats. Mid Rats, Midnight rations, is a meal for those going on the 11-7 shift or those coming off the 3-11 shift. I showed him the envelope and shared some of what Judy had written. For whatever reason, she decided I was an OK sailor. She even sent me a picture since I had sent her one of me with my first letter. Wow, even my picture did not scare her off.

Over the next four months, Mark and I would visit when we could. Every other Saturday was a work detail in the clinic, and I occasionally had both evening and night duty. Other than that, my hours were pretty regular. Mark, on the other hand, worked rotating shifts and worked every other weekend. We would eat together when our schedules allowed, repeated stories our girlfriends had shared. We wrote letters, read, and listened to music. We had two radio stations in Jacksonville. One played Southern Gospel all day. The other played country music during the day, but it was rock and roll from 6 to 9 in the evening, only Monday through Friday. It was all country music on the weekend. There was a rec area with vending machines and a television. We would occasionally sit in there and watch the Dean Martin Show while sipping on a Coke. I even tried to teach Mark how to play Cribbage, the card game my grandfather taught me. I gave up. Not because he couldn't learn. He kept beating the crap out of me.

Four months after my first letter, Judy and I decided it was time to meet. We had gotten to know one another through letters and phone calls, but there was no substitute for personal contact. I decided it would be easiest if I rode the bus. I learned the only bus line serving Dayton, Ohio, was Greyhound, while the only bus line serving Jacksonville, NC, was Trailways. So I bought a round-trip ticket from

Jacksonville to Dayton with a bus change in Cincinnati. I gave Judy my itinerary and approximate arrival time. We agreed I would call her when I got to the bus terminal in Dayton.

The Trailways bus made some stops along the way. At one stop, we had to change buses. The new bus had some problems. I say obviously because twice, the men on the bus had to get out and push the dang thing! Each time we pushed it to the side of the road. The first time, we got the bus started again and rolled on only to have it stop again. So off we got and pushed it aside, only this time the bus was dead. We waited for a half-hour or so until a new bus arrived. We moved the luggage from one bus to the other, and then we were on our way. Although more stops were scheduled, we did not stop again because we were so far behind schedule until we hit Cincinnati.

I waited until my bags were offloaded and then headed around the corner to the Greyhound station. The new bus was non-stop to Dayton, only it did make scheduled stops once inside the Dayton city limits.

"Apple Street," the driver said and repeated, "Apple Street."

I could see this big building with the sign Miami Valley Hospital facing the road. "This is my stop. I need to get off," I announced to the driver.

"Sorry, son. You checked your luggage. You have to stay on until we hit the depot." I sadly watched the hospital roll by, knowing my girlfriend was waiting there for me. When I did get to the depot and collected my bag, I found a payphone, put the quarter in, and called the dorm. Judy did not answer, but she was nearby.

"Hello," she said a little hesitantly.

"It's me," I said. "I am here at the station."

"Good. Linda and I will be right there."

Two girls entered the station about ten minutes later. They saw me and came right over. I was sitting but stood when they came up to me.

"Are you Steve?" one of the girls asked.

"Yes," I answered, knowing the girl who asked was not Judy.

"I'm Linda," and pushing her friend forward, "and this is Judy." We smiled and gave each other a tentative hug. We boarded a city bus back to Apple Street, and the girls talked non-stop. And they asked a lot of questions. When we arrived at the dorm, we found her parents standing in front of a large window in a common area.

"This is my mom," Judy said, pointing to the woman.

"Margaret," she said. "Welcome. I am glad to meet you."

"Thank you," I said. "I am glad to meet you."

Pointing to a tall man, Judy said, "And, this is my dad."

"So, you are the sailor boy that has come all the way from North Carolina to meet my daughter." Judy's dad worked for Goodyear Tire and Rubber in St. Mary's. This way before OSHA, earplugs, and all that. As a result, Howard, Judy's dad, had some difficulty hearing. I also learned he had two speaking volumes. Loud and louder. He also had gigantic hands the engulfed mine when we shook. He smiled the whole time.

"Yes, sir. I'm Steve." To say I was a bit intimidated would have been an understatement.

Riding the hour to St. Mary's, Judy and I sat in the back, holding hands. and trying to talk. Her parents had a lot to say and a hundred questions, which they asked on the trip. I don't know if they were curious or trying to protect their daughter from this strange sailor boy who suddenly showed up. But, of course, it did not help much when Howard, a staunch Republican, learned I was raised in a unionized, Democrat family.

The time went by quickly, and we had a good time. Judy's parents did give us some alone time, but not too much. I met her brother Dick, his family, and Judy's high school friends, Tom and Joyce. Dick drove us back to Dayton; he dropped me off at the bus station before returning his sister to her dorm. I boarded the bus to Cincinnati, where I went around the corner and caught the Trailways. No breakdowns on the way home, thank goodness. I caught a cab to the main gate and the base bus for the ride to the hospital. I checked in at the main desk and then headed over to the barracks. It was after midnight, and I did not want to disturb anyone.

"I'm awake," came a voice from the darkness across the hall. "Tell me about the trip."

The first words out of my mouth were, "I think I have just met my future wife." He laughed, and we talked for fifteen minutes. Unfortunately, he had the 7-3 shift and was gone before I got up in the morning. So I got dressed, ate breakfast, and was at the clinic a few minutes early. The other two techs peppered me with questions about my trip and meeting Judy. Dr. Kelly rarely got involved in the lives of his staff, but Dr. Charlie Brown was different. He, too, wanted to know all about my trip and meeting my girlfriend for the first time.

The first night back, I had to call home and tell my parents all about my adventure to St. Mary's, Ohio. Of course, they had the same questions everyone else had about the trip, Judy and her parents. My dad could not stop laughing when I told him we had to push the bus, not once but twice.

It took two or three days, but things settled back to normal, and then it was Mark's turn to go home. It was Valentine's Day, and Mark wanted to spend the holiday with Linda. It was after midnight when Mark got back from leave. He came in and woke me up.

"I asked Linda to marry me,"

"Good. And?"

"And she said yes!" said an excited Mark. He said that she came with him and his parents bringing him back, and they were at a motel.

"Great. Maybe we can all spend some time together tomorrow. When does your family have to go back?"

"No can do. I got orders to Nam. I am to report to FMF training tomorrow morning. They don't know, so I have to go and break the news to them now."

"Stop by the clinic before you leave," I said.

"Have to. I need to pick up my dental chart."

Mark came by the clinic. He had an examination and cleaning then left. I assisted Dr. Kelly in a mandible reduction, A marine had an auto accident, broke his lower jaw, and we were wiring it shut. Unfortunately, I was tied up with Dr. Kelly and never got to see or talk to Mark.

The Marines are a part of the Navy, and we supply them with Hospital Corpsmen, Dental Technicians, and Chaplains. Enlisted personnel assigned to the Marines must complete FMF or Fleet Marine Force training before being assigned to a unit. Mark knew what unit he would be assigned, and the unit would eventually be heading to Vietnam. Unfortunately, he did not have the time or luxury of a writing desk while in FMF training or after transferring to his unit. Consequently, whatever writing Mark did was to his family and Linda. I got one letter telling me he had arrived for training, and he did not know how much time he would have to write. After that, I never heard from Mark again.

One July afternoon, Judy noticed Linda's pastor was in the nursing school's dorm and went inside the director's office. She could not find Linda and eventually learned that Linda had gone home. Judy was told Mark had been killed in Vietnam, and Linda went to be with her family and Mark's family. As luck would have it, I was on night duty again when Judy called the hospital trying to reach me. The operator patched the call through to a payphone in the hall, and Judy gave me the news.

When I answered, expecting some excitement, I found Judy distraught, "Mark's gone," she said.

"What?" I stammered. "What do you mean gone? Where did he go?"

"Mark is dead. He was killed in Vietnam," she managed to get out.

"How? When?" I wanted to know.

"A helicopter crash, I think," Judy said. "I don't know much else."

We talked and consoled each other for a few more minutes, and then the call was over.

The remaining time I spent at Lejeune, I would monitor the number of corpsmen I had known or treated at the hospital being sent to Vietnam and coming home in a box. I found one or two marines who were either there when the helicopter went down or part of Mark's unit. I told Judy about one Marine who said he was part of Mark's unit, and he did not believe Mark was supposed to be on that helicopter. Judy and I decided not to share this with the family and add to their grieving process.

I would learn from another marine who was part of Mark's unit and said Mark was always assigned to the operation, but another medic was not. It doesn't matter much now. Both were on the helicopter, and both died.

Shortly after the news of Mark's death, I was promoted to E-5, second-class petty officer. There was room for only one E-5 in the clinic, so two years and five days after arriving at Camp Lejeune, I was becoming a tin-can sailor. Tin cans are what we called destroyers and supporting crafts. I would be on two Destroyer Tenders and a destroyer leader, also known as a frigate. The war was raging half a world away, and the news was a precious commodity. Mark was dead, and I put him out of my mind. With the USS. Norfolk (DL1), I spent seven months visiting twenty ports in Central and South America. My final deployment was four weeks in Miami, Florida.

Within a two-week period in August 1968, I got married, was discharged from the Navy, honeymooned in New York City, moved to Dayton, Ohio, and started classes at the University of Dayton. In that order! Judy took me to Miamisburg, and we visited Mark's grave. By this time, Linda was working in Cincinnati and kept in touch with Judy through letters and phone calls. Neither of us knew Mark's family. We were newlyweds, and I was starting classes at the University of Dayton. Between the Navy and our honeymoon, I missed all freshman orientation activities and was struggling to find my way around campus on my own.

Mark had been dead about two years, and everyone was moving on. The one concession we agreed on was the naming of our first son. His first name would be Mark, in honor of Mark Dennis.

CHAPTER 3
Volunteering

The trouble with oral history is the quality of the information and the inability to cite a specific reference by author, title, and page. For example, I heard Mark volunteered for Vietnam through a story his brother told me during the filming of *Unsolved Mysteries*. When I began to write this book, a story in the *Tampa Bay News* quoted Mark's last remaining sister who said Mark volunteered for Vietnam from the carrier U.S.S. Wasp. This information threw me for a loop since there is nothing in the hundreds of pages of information Jerry gave me that puts Mark on board an aircraft carrier.

His cousin then shared with me, "Mark volunteered for Vietnam when he enlisted in the Navy. Mark said it was his duty to serve."

The only consistent thread is Mark told his parents, family, and friends he volunteered for Vietnam. I told my parents the same thing. I told them I had volunteered for Vietnam. But, while Mark did eventually sacrifice his life for his country in Vietnam, neither one of us volunteered for Vietnam.

In 1966, with hostilities escalating in Southeast Asia, the Navy was recommissioning the U.S.S. Hope, a hospital ship. Mark had been killed in Vietnam, and my younger brother was drug along the flight deck of the U.S.S. Kitty Hawk and would spend the following year in the hospital. My older brother was off the coast of Vietnam on the U.S.S. Midway. I thought it was my turn to step up to the plate and head west.

The Hope would be ported in Long Beach, California but would be deployed to the seas off the coast of Vietnam. The Navy was looking for volunteers and had specific requirements. I met those requirements and completed the chit (request form) for transfer to the ship. I filled out that chit requesting a transfer every month for four months, at which time the Navy announced they filled all positions for the ship. I was never selected. What is even more surprising with all of my requests, no one thought to tag me for FMF duty and serve with a medical battalion *in-country*, as being boots on the ground became to known. I would leave Lejeune and be assigned to three ships, all based out of Norfolk, Virginia.

Most historians mark March 1965 as the start of the Vietnam War. We had Marines guarding our diplomatic missions, as they did everywhere around the globe. Even after the French pulled out, we may have had combat troops on the ground supporting the French mission. Some of our service personnel would be killed in Vietnam, but it would be a footnote of sorts and not a blazing headline.

Mark and I graduated from high school in 1964, before the hostilities began to make news. My brother, John, graduated in 1965 and, Vietnam was very much in the news. There was even talk of reinstating the draft.

When Mark was killed in July 1966, his hometown remembered him as the first person from Miamisburg to be killed in Vietnam. So, just how did he get to be *in-country*?

Mark wanted to be a doctor, and his fiancée said he wanted to go to medical school at the University of Cincinnati. So, like me, he enlisted under the Hospitalman program. The Navy guaranteed him training as either a dental technician or a hospital corpsman. I went the dental tech route, and Mark became a corpsman. This happened in 1964, about nine months before the official start of the war.

Mark may have shared a desire to go to Vietnam with his recruiter and possibly had that tour of duty in the back of his head when he signed his enlistment papers. He could not have volunteered at that time because the Navy wanted to know if he would be one of the 5%

who washed out or one of the 95% who graduated. He technically did not have a MOS or Military Occupation Specialty. Your MOS determines where you will be assigned once your training is complete. And since we had not officially entered a war status with the North Vietnamese, serving in Vietnam was not an option.

Near the end of his training as a hospital corpsman, he would have been asked to select three desired duty stations. I picked Rota, Spain, London, England, and ship duty. Instead, the Navy assigned me to the Naval Hospital and Camp Lejeune. You don't always get what you want. Being close to his family, I would imagine Mark picked duty stations along the east coast.

Again, the war in Vietnam had not yet begun, and I doubt FMF duty, which is the only sure ticket to Vietnam, was considered by Mark. Whatever his choices were, he got my preferred duty. He was on board a ship in the Mediterranean, the U.S.S. Wasp, seeing some sights I longed to see. However, while Mark was on board, the mission of the Wasp changed. The ship was to become the primary recovery vessel for the fledgling space program. The change in mission required going into dry-dock for new equipment and upgrades. Non-essential personnel, including corpsmen, were transferred off the ship and Mark wound up at Camp Lejeune.

I arrived first and Mark a few weeks later, but we learned most of the personnel spent their entire enlistment there. The war in Vietnam was just cranking up but was still a vague thought somewhere at the back of our minds. Mark was one of the first of many corpsmen to have their time at the hospital cut short for assignment to FMF duty. Mark was one of the first of many corpsmen I knew and served with to find their names on the obituary page of the *Stars and Stripes*.

When we did *Unsolved Mysteries*, Jerry told the story several times that Mark volunteered to go so a married medic wouldn't.

According to Jerry, "Mark was at the end of his Marine training when he learned of a married medic having orders to go to Vietnam. Mark volunteered to take his place."

I told Jerry then the Navy does not work that way. The Navy would consider wanting sea/shore duty to be closer to home for medical reasons or similar reasons for a change. However, under no circumstances would the Navy consider a request so a specific person would not have to go.

In the end, does it make a difference whether Mark volunteered? And if he did not volunteer, why tell the story? In the end, it does not matter if Mark was assigned or volunteered. Either way, he went to Vietnam. While there, he was killed. He did not come home. The story speaks volumes about who Mark was as a sailor and as a man. He knew his parents and his family were struggling with his heading into harm's way. Everyone knew it, but I doubt anyone verbalized the fear that Mark might die over there. It was not a case of bravado; of Mark beating his chest a la Tarzan. As was his nature, Mark was humble, contrite, and considerate of others. He was letting his family know he was alright with whatever the future held. He wanted them to support him and his new mission in the Navy. And they did.

Whether by choice or by fate, Mark achieved the goal he shared with his family. Hopefully, he could spare a married medic and his family the horrors of war through his choice. At least, I would like to think he had.

CHAPTER 4
Sea Knight

*The military has a profane term for what occurred on July 15, 1966. They call it a "Cluster F**k!" I have read multiple accounts of that day when a CH-46 Sea Knight was hit by enemy fire, crashed, and burned, killing one crew member and fourteen passengers. This account is a reasonable facsimile of what happened that hot July afternoon near Quang Tri Provence, South Vietnam.*

When I met Jerry in Washington, D.C., to film our episode, he was excited to share with me what he knew and suspected. He gave me a name for the style of the helicopter, a name that I do not recall.

"Mark's helicopter was a Chinook," he told me. Whenever he referred to Mark's helicopter, he referred to it as a Chinook. As I began to put this book together, I had a friend of mine correct me. He served in the same position Sgt. Gary Lucas did; he was a gunner on multiple missions.

"The Army flew Chinook Ch-47s. Marines flew Ch-46 Sea Knights." My friend corrected me. "They are slightly smaller," he told me when I asked about the difference.

"Think about the Chevy Suburban and the Chevy Tahoe," he said. "General Motors make both; both are SUVs, and both have essentially the same profile. However, the Tahoe is smaller."

Both the Chinook and the Sea Knight are massive, dual rotor helicopters made by a division of Boeing Aircraft. Only the larger Army version is referred to as a Chinook. The smaller version made for the

Navy and the Marines is called the Sea Knight. Both have the same profile, and from a distance or standing alone, the casual observer would not be able to distinguish between the two.

Regardless of the differences, both are massive aircraft capable of moving large numbers of troops, equipment, and supplies. They were the workhorse of the military during Vietnam. However, the terrain comprised hills and jungles, and creating runways for fixed-wing aircraft capable of completing the same mission was not practical.

There are times in the summer when airliners are unable to take off because of the temperatures. It gets hot, and there is insufficient air for these massive, multi-ton aircraft to take off. The same applies to these helicopters. The super-heated atmosphere not augmented by wind cannot provide the energy need to put one of the whirlybirds in the air.

Dong Ha was a major staging area about 30 to 40 minutes from Quang Tri. Quang Tri was one of the northernmost Marine outposts comprised of hills, valleys, and jungles. The northern boundary of the outpost is the Demilitarized Zone or DMZ. Therefore, in theory, we would not shoot into the DMZ, nor would the North Vietnamese shoot from the DMZ. However, in May and June 1966, the NVA began encroaching on this area, and in July, we decided to launch an offensive that would push the NVA back north of the DMZ. This operation was dubbed "Operation Hastings."

The landing zone for the Sea Knights was identified as LZ Crow. Most LZs were designed to accommodate up to five Ch-46s at one time. By this standard, LZ Crow was small. It could accommodate up to four choppers at one time, but this required both precision and luck. Many Sea Knights were lost due to mid-air collision, dodging debris from such collisions or misjudging conditions and coming in too high, too fast, or both, thereby overshooting the LZ and finding themselves entangled in the jungle.

The NVA did not go quietly back north of the DMZ, and the sector became known as "hot," meaning gun and artillery fire was exchanged with the enemy. Those in charge decided to provide more than 100 additional combat units to the base.

On the morning of July 15, sixteen Sea Knights assembled at Dong Ha. The code name for the operation was "Rose," and each chopper carried the designation Rose-1 through Rose-16. They would go into Quang Tri in flights of four. The first four would fly in, discharge their Marines, and fly out as quickly as possible. The next four would repeat the process until all four flights and 16 Sea Knights had flown in, landed, discharged their passengers, and returned to Dong Ha.

Rose-1 through Rose-4 loaded up and headed out for the 40-minute flight to Quang Tri. These four approached Quang Tri from the west and arrived without incident. The choppers flew with the rear ramp partially deployed, reducing time and vulnerability on the ground. Rose-1, Rose-2, and Rose-3 landed and discharged their passengers without incident. As Rose-4 approached the LZ, the wind shifted, and now the chopper was too high and coming in too fast to reach the LZ safely. They overshot the zone and landed in the Jungle. They relayed the problem to the rest of the choppers and moved from the west to the south. The new approach took them over dense jungle where any enemy troops would be hidden from view by the jungle canopy.

The change in heading did not significantly change the flight experience until Rose-5 was about five minutes away. Enemy ground fire erupted.

"Abort! Abort! Abort! Rose-5 says all units Abort!"

Rose 5 repeated this multiple times as Rose-5 took evasive action to avoid being hit and possibly downed by the enemy. Finally, rose-7 and Rose-8, heading the warning, managed to abort the mission and head back to Dong Ha. Rose-5, 6, and 7 related the status of the LZ to their home base, and the remaining eight choppers remained on the ground.

Before Rose-6 could take evasive action, one or more incendiary rounds hit a fule tank.

Side gunner Gary Lucas would recall, "We were immediately engulfed with waist-high flames and heavy smoke. The troops were buckled in their basket seats with nowhere to go."

Any marine sucking in air to scream and yell in terror and agony was silenced by the scorching temperature of the air and the oxygen-robbing thick smoke. The helicopter was at 1500 feet when it was hit and dropped almost immediately to a tree-top height of about 40 feet.

The cockpit of Rose-6 was immediately engulfed with the thick smoke, intensifying whenever it slowed to land. The makers of the Sea Knight designed it for vertical lift and land. The makers never envisioned the need for a running landing. It had to stop its forward movement before descending. It was those times when the smoke became so thick, and the forward movement had to be reinstated.

With his head hanging out the starboard side, copilot Richey hollered to his captain, "I think I've got it. We've overrun the LZ, but I see a clearing I think I can hit."

"You got it!" yelled the captain and turned controls over to Richey.

For Lucas, the few minutes between being hit and finally hitting the ground were an eternity. In his statement for *Unsolved Mysteries,* Lucas would recall, *I saw an individual run off the helicopter ramp, and his clothing was smoking.* Then Lucas recounts, *I saw a second man jump from the aircraft. He was on fire at the time. Shortly after that, we hit the ground, and I always felt the aircraft probably fell on that man."*

From here forward, things get confusing as stories vary, even among the three survivors. Most, if not all, of this, may be attributed to the time elapsing between the time they crashed and the time they gave their statements. What facts the Navy provided them in prepping them for their statements, if any, is unknown. Just as Jerry had to help me recall what we had discussed two decades previously, I am sure the Navy may have provided these witnesses with specific facts to facilitate their recollection of the events.

In his statement, Lucas says *I found the crew chief was still alive, but his leg from the knee down was pinned between the aircraft and ground, and he had also been hit by around. When I was attempting to pull him free, he was hit by other rounds in the back and died.* Captain McAlister tells a slightly different story in his statement. *I was momentarily pinned in the cockpit but managed to free myself and exit. (copilot) Richey exited by the copilot's emergency hatch, followed by me. Lucas went back into the compartment to see if anyone there could be helped. He told me later he saw no one alive, so he got out. We walked a short distance up the hill, and within 1 to 3 minutes, the aircraft exploded and burned for several hours.* In the book *Bonnie Sue*, Richey tells author Marion Sturkey yet a different story. Richey stated he saw Telfer jump out of the opening, and the Sea Knight rolled on top of him, killing him. As for Lucas, Richey recalls *Grunts had found Lucas huddled in the jungle, in shock, and unable to speak 50 meters from the fire. His fire-resistant flight suit, although burned in places, had saved his life.* Sturkey notes Telfer was KIA with **NOBODY RECOVERED.**

According to Sturkey, they did not recover Telfer's body, yet I have a Certificate of Death for Telfer stating he was identified by dog tags and dental charts with no notation other than burns. If partially buried, his leg(s) below the knee should show some sign of a multi-ton aircraft pinning him down. Richey says the helicopter rolled over and buried him. Lucas said he attempted to pull him from under the aircraft, and after noticing Tefler was dead, Lucas observed a large hole in his back – not noted on the death certificate.

And what about Lucas? Lucas said he was unconscious for a short period of time, noticed both pilot and copilot gone, and discovered Telfer pinned by one leg below the knee under the aircraft. He attempted to rescue his friend while under fire. Telfer was shot several times in the back, but Lucas never admitted being shot. McAlister says he, Richey, and Lucas all left together and were together when the helicopter exploded and burned. Sturkey says Lucas was found alone, in the jungle, in shock, and unable to speak.

Lucas was right; two men jumped from the helicopter after being hit. I have read several reports and talked to veterans who witnessed people jumping from helicopters. I have seen a photograph of Mark's helicopter after being hit with a marine jumping or falling from the aircraft. Lucas always believed the Sea Knight landed on the second jumper, but he was incorrect. Over the years, as the records have been cleaned up, we now know the names of the two jumpers. In addition, we now have two more men identified as being on that craft, which means 14 Marines were on board and not 12 as previously believed If Lilly and Morris were the two who jumped, then where did Mark go?

The burning of the helicopter as described is inconsistent with the death certificates Jerry provided me. Based on everything I have been able to find out about the temperature of the fire in that helicopter and the duration it was to have burned, no identification through dental records would have been possible. The fire in the helicopter from the JP3 fuel could have easily approached over 3,000 F. This would have made dental comparison impossible. Dog tags would have melted. Yet ten of those identified used identification tags as a form of identification. Dental charts identified eight. None of them have reports of bullets or grenade fragments.

#

There were fourteen passengers on that Rose-5 when it left Dong Ha and not the dozen as anticipated. 2nd Lt. Ronald Culler and Cpl. James Reid, both of engineer battalions, hitched a ride for sightseeing. Perhaps there was a campaign ribbon involved, or maybe just for fun. We'll never know, but they were unlisted passengers on that craft.

After being hit, we now know Lilly and Morris jumped. The altitude and airspeed are undetermined. They may have died upon impact. It is also possible they died shortly afterward from their wounds suffered from the inferno that was once Rose-5.

A dozen Marines were on board; they collected a dozen dog tags. One fatality was known to be a crew member, leaving eleven tags. As a result, the first estimate of 11 passengers on board was made. However, Lilly's and Morris's units added them to the casualty list, raising the total number on board to thirteen. The assumption became 13 killed with three survivors. At some point, it was determined that Mark was on board but not accounted for, and this whole mess began.

I must question Lucas' recollection of events because Telfer is shot multiple times in the back, but Lucas, working right next to and sometimes behind him, and Lucas is never hit. I think Richey's account is accurate, but the identification was wrong. Mark was still alive, or barely alive, when the chopper came to rest on the side of the hill. Mark was not tethered, and the jolt threw him out of the helicopter just as it rolled, burying Mark under the fuselage. Not expecting anyone other than the crew chief to be at that opening, Richey made the connection and concluded Telfer was the one buried by the massive aircraft.

As far as Telfer's notation of *No Body Recovered*, that is just one more case of the military's lack of attention to detail. Richey may have told his story to someone who told someone who had someone make out a casualty card with that notation. Since remains were identified as Telfer's by dog tags and dental records, I am confident they recovered his body.

In 2008 records were cleaned up, and it was determined Lilly and Morris were incorrectly identified as ground casualties. The mistake was easy to make. They recovered the bodies some distance from the final resting place of Rose-6. Checking of the records put them on the aircraft on that fateful day.

Granted, this is pure conjecture and speculation on my part, but it fits the facts reported over the years, how we went from 11 casualties to 15, and how two people jumped without Mark being one of them. More importantly, how Mark wound up underneath the CH-46 Sea Knight, call signal Rose-5.

*Courtesy of the Dennis
Family*

THE FINAL FLIGHT

HMM-265, MAG-18

Sgt. Robert R. Telfer, Fonda, NY

A CO. IST ENG BN

2nd Lt. Ronald K. Cullers, Shelbina, MO

B CO, 3RD ENG BN

Cpl. James M. Reid, Philadelphia, PA

E CO, 2ND BN, 1ST MARINES

SSgt. Herolin T. Simmons, Ahoskie, NC (Silver Star 4/29/66)

Cpl. Orson H. Case, Johnstown, NY

HM3 Andrew P. Chamaj, Scenery Hill, PA

Cpl. Paul R. Chambers, Scottsboro, AL

Pfc. James W. Herrick, New York, NY

Pfc. Michael A. Cunnion, Mount Vernon, NY

Pfc. Michael A. Gooden, Bellflower, CA
PFC Carl W. Schloemer, Belfontaine Neighbors, MO
Pfc. Gerald E. Stubstad, Chicago, IL

H&S CO. 2ND BN, 1ST MARINES
HM3 Mark V. Dennis

H&S CO, 3RD BN, 4TH MARINES
Cpl. William J. Lilly, Rowayton, CT
HN John N. Morris, Meldrin, GA

CHAPTER 5
Identifying Mark

"As a matter of fact, all of the remains from the crash were recovered."
Lt. Cmdr. James Cole
"Unsolved Mysteries" 1990

Dennis, Mark V.
7789145
HM3

Identification was established through a check with all units concerned in regards to the actual passengers aboard the aircraft. Complete identification made on all other deceased with on DENNIS remaining, and one cadaver.
Identity was established in that manner.

Three things must first occur to have Mark identified in this manner.

First, the government must

1. establish a firm number and identity of passengers on the heli-copter at the time of the crash.
2. Second, the number of corpses must match the number of known deceased.
3. Third, before ruling identification through elimination, they must identify all other casualties.

There were six units onboard the Sea Knight on that fateful day in July 1966.

- HMM-265, Mag-16 (1)
- A Co, 1st Eng Bn (1)
- B Co, 3rd Eng Bn (1)
- E Co, 2dn Bn, 1st Marines (9)
- H&S Co, 2nd Bn, 1st Marines (1)
- H&S Co, 3rd Bn, 4th Marines (2)

A total of 18 Marines perished that day, including three ground forces. However, two we now know were on the helicopter when it went down were misclassified as ground casualties, giving a false reading of the number of marines on board.

Additionally, over the years, the official number fluctuated between 1970 when Jerry exhumed the body and 1990 when we recorded the "Missing Medic."

"My phone has been tapped from time to time," Jerry told me.

"How do you know?" I asked with skepticism.

"Easy, I said I talked to Lucas and changed the number of people on board at the time of the crash."

"Really?" I asked in surprise.

"Yup. A few days later, I got a phone call saying they may have miscounted the passengers and gave me the number Lucas and I agreed upon."

It is hard to have confidence in the findings when the facts are so easily changed. To change the numbers involved as new information is gained is not a significant issue in and of itself. However, when they used that number to identify a missing servicemember, any change became monumental.

CPL Lilly and HN Morris were erroneously listed as ground casualties. However, that information had changed to reflect they were killed when the helicopter was downed by enemy fire. Thus, the military was using incomplete data when they identified an unknown corpse as Mark Dennis.

Every passenger must be found and accounted for. This means there should have been 18 bodies in the morgue from that day's hostilities. Before identifying Mark through the process of elimination, 17 cadavers would have had to be positively identified. We now know the maximum number of remains to be recovered could not exceed 17. Because the helicopter hid one body under its massive frame, there is no possible way for those on-site to have retrieved everyone killed that day. We don't know if Mark was alone under the chopper or if one or more marines suffered the same fate. Even if it was only Mark buried and out of sight, it would have been possible to have recovered all of the bodies and had everyone positively identified except on body.

Without the number recovered matching the number of those killed, it is physically impossible to identify anyone through the elimination process. Therefore, the best outcome is a listing of "Missing and presumed dead." If Mark had company in the dirt under the chopper, each should have the same notation: "Missing and presumed dead." If this had been the notation, perhaps it would not have taken 48 years to excavate the crash site and find these fallen heroes.

The third point is moot. We know the Navy did not have a firm manifest of the people on the downed Sea Knight. We also know Quang Tri marines couldn't recover all fatalities from that day. No one found Mark's dog tags because they were with him, hidden under the fuselage of a downed Sea Knight.

Setting aside the current knowledge which makes a process of elimination identification impossible, let us examine the facts provided by the Navy and used to make the identification.

DATE OF DEATH: Except for 2nd Lt. Culler, every death certificate has the wrong date of death. We know the Sea Knight went down on 15 July 66; the date on the remaining dozen certificates all has 17 July 66. Two certificates shave the date and the time of death. One says 0300 (3:00 am), and another says 1800 (6:00 pm).

CORRECTED DATES: All but two death certificates have an updated date of death in the summary box on the back of the certificate. Mark Dennis has the incorrect date of death as 17 July 66, and there is no corrected date on the reverse. CPL Reid has an updated date of death of 16 July 66, which is still not the correct date of the incident.

IDENTIFICATION: Of the twelve positively identified, nine were identified through dental records. Fire can make identification through dental records anywhere from difficult to impossible, depending on the temperature of the fire. Teeth may discolor, filling materials may shrink, melt, change shape or crack. In extreme heat, teeth have been known to disintegrate. The fact that so many of the remains were identified by dental charts tells me the temperature was severe enough to scorch and burn flesh but not so high as to impact the dentition significantly. The short duration of the fire may also explain why there were no spontaneous detonations involved. Two, Reid and Cullers, were identified by dog tags alone. There is no indication of how PFC Gooden was identified. There is no mention of dog tags nor identification using dental records. Therefore, there is a complete absence of any information on how they determined the identity of this marine.

2ND LT. CULLERS: This death certificate is particularly troublesome. It is signed and dated 12 August 1966, or about the time Mark was being lowered into the ground. The summary section says *This Certificate of Death has been prepared from the information contained in a signed* *and incomplete NAVMED-N received from 3ʳᵈ Med Bn, 3ʳᵈ Mardiv (Rein) FMF, and the decedent's health records.* There is no notation of what was incomplete regarding the original NAVMED-N, nor when it was initially signed. There is no way to establish whether the initial identification was made before or after the identification of Mark Dennis. It almost reads as if someone corrected it at some point after the funeral. Instead of saying "burned" as a reason for no fingerprints, it says, "Not Obtainable." If the entire body were burned, the scars noted in the description would not have been observable.

    SGT TELFER: The anomaly with this death certificate is minor but still worth mentioning. Telfer was identified on the same day as Mark Dennis. Was his identification before or after Mark's?

    Setting aside the fluctuating number of persons on the helicopter and accepting the number of 13 fatalities from the aircraft, the process of elimination identification remains invalid. It was physically impossible for the marines at Quang Tri on that day to have recovered all remains. We know this because at least one was found beneath the Sea Knight when they finally excavated the helicopter. Assuming Mark was the only one found under the wreckage, only 17 bodies could have been recovered of the 18 known fatalities. The only way a body believed to be that of Mark Dennis had to be recovered from somewhere other than Quang Tri or a different date's hostilities. However, the language used in revealing the results of the excavation suggests they recovered a single corpse.

*Courtesy of the Dennis
Family*

REMEMBERING MY COUSIN

Mark V Dennis was my cousin. We were the two youngest of the cousins. Mark was an incredible person. He was quiet and humble. He was caring and gentle. One of his Navy buddies told me that Mark never spent money on himself, but he would spend it on his buddies if they needed money. Mark was not only a huge loss to our family, but he was a huge loss to humanity. I will see you in heaven one day, Mark. I love you.

LINDA ERWIN

CHAPTER 6
The Nightmare Begins

In 1970, *Newsweek* magazine did a photo-essay of the Vietnam War. Included in this essay was a photograph of what the magazine called "an unidentified POW." Had this picture (a) not been published or (b) had this picture not been seen by the Dennis family, none of what follows would have happened. Instead, the family would have lived out their lives knowing their son and brother died for his country and the United States military had given Mark the full honor and respect due to being a fallen sailor.

However, the photograph was both published and seen by the Dennis family. To this day, looking at only that one photograph, there is a strong resemblance to HM3 Mark V. Dennis. For the first time, the family began to consider their son might have mistakenly been listed killed in action when he was a prisoner of war held by the North Vietnamese in an unspecified location. It was then Jerry Dennis, Mark's only brother, launched a fifty-one-year fight with the government over what was the truth about Mark. Was he alive or dead? If he is dead, is that his body in the grave with his headstone? If he is alive, where is he?

Jerry opened the box in 1970 and would die on the operating table in 2002 of an abdominal aortic aneurysm. The box would be closed in 2017. The grief the United States Government knowingly and willingly inflicted on this family is unthinkable. At the same time, Jerry and his family were impatient for the truth. The wheels of the government sometimes turn so slowly as to appear not to be moving at all. Acting without the blessings and assistance of the government, the family struck out on their own.

In trying to understand what the family did and how they accomplished it, I have talked with several funeral directors. The rules in 1966 were still being written when it came to the remains of fallen heroes. Jerry and his family were not the first to ignore protocol and strike out on their own. The Dennis family was not the only one to find a nightmare waiting in the casket brought up from the grave. It is hard for the funeral directors I visited with to give me answers because what Jerry did would not be possible today. The remains of one buried with military honors may not be raised without the blessing and authority of the Department of Defense. And if, as in the case with Mark Dennis, the DOD says the family will not view the remains, the family wishes do not count. The family will not view the remains. In fact, in those cases where the DOD determines the remains are not to be viewed, the casket is not just locked, it is glued shut, and no one will open it. This information is from a funeral director in Killeen, Texas, who has handled too many funerals for soldiers killed on active duty.

The 1960s were much more innocent than today. Especially in the early to mid-60s. By the late 60s, the Vietnam war was raging in full view of everyone. For the first time, war was not a series of sanitized photographs in a magazine; it was brought into homes, especially at dinner time, live, and in living color. The Vietnam war did not have a front or a rear. It only had a here. It was reminiscent of our revolutionary war. Only the roles were reversed. When we fought for our independence, the British wore bright colors, marched in formation, and followed a rulebook. The colonists had no uniform, very little formal training, and were difficult for the British soldiers to identify. In Vietnam, the United States wore a distinctive uniform, marched in formation, and followed basic rules. The Viet Cong, as we called the enemy, were peasants and farmers. They had no uniform and followed no basic set of rules. It signaled the end to ethical warfare if there ever is such a thing. If there was an age of innocence, the Vietnam War signaled its demise.

Whistler painted a picture of an old woman better known as "Whistler's Mother." Whistler titled this picture, *A Study in Black and White.* This photograph, titled by *Newsweek* magazine, *A Photo of an*

Unidentified POW, might also be titled, *A Study in White and Black.* The predominant color in the black and white photograph is white. The wall is white with some obscured writing in black; we see black letters. The POW is sitting on a white mattress with a darker bedframe. His hair color is black, as are the shadows. But the POW is dressed in white, and his skin tones are white. The color of the cell bars is unclear. They may be grey or painted white.

The first time I saw the photograph was when we were filming the "Missing Medic" episode of *Unsolved Mysteries.* A copy of the picture is included in the hundreds of pages of narrative, photos, and documents Jerry gave me detailing Jerry's fight to get Mark's status changed to Missing in Action (MIA). Mark's father, "Uncle Pete," as Mark's cousin called him, discovered the photograph. He called other family members and encouraged them to get a copy and look at the picture. According to Jerry, Anne, Mark's sister, fainted when she saw the picture.

As far as everyone was concerned, the photo was Mark, their deceased son and brother they laid to rest four years previous. As I looked at the picture, the pose was familiar to me as I had seen Mark sit on the edge of his bunk at Lejeune in the same way. Assuming the role of family spokesperson, Jerry agreed to draft a letter and send it to the Navy with the family's concerns. They waited to hear back.

Jerry ended his tale with, "The Navy said the POW in the photo was not Mark, but a previously identified Navy POW."

Jerry added something about the family wanting privacy and left me with the impression the Navy never identified the POW for him. Jerry became convinced there was a conspiracy to avoid making Mark an MIA. The photo played a prominent role in the presentation of the "Missing Medic" episode. I do not know if Jerry told the producers at *Unsolved Mysteries,* but he never mentioned to me the republication of the photo in another national magazine, *Life,* with POW identified as Navy pilot, Paul Galanti. It would be three decades later. As I began researching this book, I discovered the truth. But the story does not end there.

An internet search of Mark Dennis POW/MIA produced many informational sites, and many included the photo of the 'unidentified' POW. Sometimes the picture is tied to a photograph of Mark with no mention of Paul Galanti. The implication is the photo might be that of Mark.

Conversely, an internet search for Paul Galanti POW/MIA produces several information sites. First, the photo is there with Galanti, with him identified as the POW pictured. Second, when Paul was still held prisoners by the North Vietnamese, his wife featured the photo in a letter-writing campaign to get him home.

I don't know if Jerry ever attempted to reach out to the Galanti family. Bryan Curtis, Jerry and Mark's nephew, is the new spokesman for the family, and he told me he had had a conversation with Paul. The controversy over Mark's status was still raging, but Brian told me he, after talking with Paul and seeing other pictures of Galanti as a POW.

Whether the Navy told Jerry the identity of the POW pictured or not, Jerry used the picture to justify opening *Pandora's Box*. Jerry decided to take on the United States Government to get his kid brother's status changed to MIA. But, unfortunately, it would prove to be a lengthy and costly venture that he would not see to its conclusion.

The identity of that POW has now become a moot point. Information I uncovered while researching this book proved the photograph was not Mark Dennis, but more importantly, it could not have been Mark. That photograph may have been the spark giving life to this controversy. But, it in no way justifies the humiliation and grief to which this family has been subjected.

*Courtesy of the Dennis
Family*

UNCLE MARK

Mark Dennis was my mother's youngest brother (Karen Anne Dennis). I was 3 years old when he was killed, and I clearly remember the moment my mother was notified by the Navy in person at my grandmother's house, which was directly across the street from our house in Miamisburg. It is one of my first memories in my life, and I can never forget it. Jerry, Mark's brother, died while trying to find the truth about the body buried in Miamisburg. I have vowed to find out with absolute certainty whether the remains are those of Mark Dennis or not. I have researched the incident, spoken to survivors and witnesses, collected photographs and stories from the incredibly brave men who were there, and saw 2 men jump from the CH 46 on 071566, Quang-tri RVN. I have also read the beautiful comments on this site, and I am truly brought to tears by how people loved this gentle, giving 19-year-old boy. I am very grateful to read such things about Mark because all I ever hear about anymore is the horrible event that ended all possibility of me and my family knowing him better. My mother told me that my uncle Mark, and his fiancée (Linda), visited us right before he left for his tour and we walked across the street to the church and flew kites.

We will know with 100% certainty very soon, thanks to modern DNA testing. God bless my uncle Mark V. Dennis, all his fellow Marines and Corpsman, and all his caring friends and family.

Bryan Curtis

CHAPTER 7
Unsolved Mysteries

Part I

I graduated from the University of Dayton in 1971 and had accepted a teaching job at Harding Junior High in Hamilton, Ohio. Hamilton is less than twenty miles north of Cincinnati, and we were beginning to think about starting a family. Judy had taken a nursing job at the hospital located just a couple of blocks from the school. We had one car, and Judy worked the 3-11 shift. Judy would take me to work and go back to our apartment. She would then drive to the school and park the car. Then, she walked the three blocks to the hospital. At 11 each night, I would go to the hospital, pick her up and bring her home.

I was unaware of the controversy over Mark's death. Judy was busy working at Miami Valley Hospital, and I was trying to get through UD in three years. Linda had moved to Cincinnati by this time, and she and Judy kept in touch with letters and phone calls. I never had the opportunity to meet any of Mark's family. Mark was gone and, while I regret it now, I never reached out to his family. We did not know of the photo in the magazine, the exhumation, or the coroner's report. Living in Hamilton, we watched the television stations broadcasting from Cincinnati, and our newspaper came from Cincinnati. While the controversy did make the newspapers in the Dayton area, we were in the dark. Until one day.

Linda called Judy and broke the news of the controversy. Linda also said Mark's brother, Jerry Dennis, need to talk to me about his brother's situation. We had not talked about Mark or his death much beyond agreeing to name our first son Mark. I did not know what Jerry wanted from me or if I had anything to tell him. Judy reminded me of the Marine I met a Lejeune saying Mark was not supposed to be on the helicopter. Mark was an important part of our lives, and I agreed to meet with Jerry and help in any way I could. Judy and Linda coordinated the meeting. We decided to meet on Thursday. Judy had the day off, and we would have time to visit.

It was just under an hour's drive from Hamilton to Miamisburg. We met Jerry and the family at Jerry's parent's house around 6:30. Judy and the family were in the dining room, sitting around the table and visiting. Linda was there, and she and Judy were sharing nursing school stories. Jerry and I were in the living room. Sitting on the couch, Jerry was bringing me up to speed with the controversy regarding Mark's death. In a small vial, there was a tooth.

"We took this tooth from the skull of the body the Navy gave us." He handed me the tooth, opened Mark's dental record, and placed the open file on the coffee table. He identified the tooth by number and pointed to the dental record. I did not question how he came to know the tooth number, but there was an inconsistency with the tooth I was holding and the dental record on the table. I examined the record, and another technician, Julia Roberts, filled out the record, stamped the doctor's name on the line, and initialed the entry. The doctor was Capt. Charles A. Brown, but before I left the hospital, Dr. Brown had been promoted to Lt. Commander and transferred. I suggested Dr. Brown was the best source of information.

Well before cell phones, the internet, and instant access to anything and everything, Jerry had somehow tracked down Dr. Brown, who was now a Commander. So Judy and I made another trip to Miamisburg, and I had the opportunity to talk with him. It was a good talk, and he said he remembered me, and I told him what we needed.

At the onset of the call, Dr. Brown said he did not have much time, and before Jerry could talk with him, he had to go. Dr. Brown did agree to talk to Jerry if he would call him and gave me the date and times that would be best. Jerry and I marveled at our good fortunes. Judy and I left and asked Jerry to call me after he talked with Dr. Brown.

Jerry did call me a few days later. Yes, he had called Dr. Brown twice, once during each time suggested by the dentist.

"He's unavailable," Jerry said in a frustrated tone. "Seems he got emergency orders and won't be available to talk for at least four months." Jerry was becoming suspicious, paranoid, and convinced of a coverup, a conspiracy, or some combination of the two.

Part II

In late 1989 or early 1990, after watching an episode of the popular reality-based television show, *Unsolved Mysteries*, Jerry Dennis thought this would be the perfect platform to get Mark's story out to the nation. Because I had helped him with an issue with a tooth pulled from the skull in 1972, he suggested me as a participant. Since assisting Jerry almost two decades earlier, I had moved twice, and my family and I now lived in the Waco, Texas, area. I had not talked to Jerry since then and was unprepared for the phone call and request.

In June 1990, our family had taken a road trip to Washington, D.C., to view the sights. We were gone for almost two weeks and visited many sights, including the Vietnam Memorial, known affectionally as "The Wall." I was unprepared for the emotions that flooded me, especially when I saw Mark's name engraved as a casualty of the war. We visited the wall twice that trip; once in the morning and then again at night. The lights illuminating the wall from the ground up were both eerie and moving. Those feelings stayed with me for a long time.

We had not been home for more than a few days when I got a call one evening.

"Hello, is this Mr. Wilcox"

"Yes."

"Mr. Steve Wilcox, a former dental tech in the Navy?"

"Yes." I was nervous and answered cautiously, stringing out my one-word answers.

"This is *Unsolved Mysteries*, and we have been talking with Mr. Jerry Dennis. We would like to do a story on his brother, Mark, and he suggested you might be willing to participate."

"I don't know," I said with some hesitancy. "It's been a long time since I have talked with Jerry, and I don't know what I might be able to contribute."

The voice continued, "We are filming in Washington, D.C. We'll provide airfare both ways, put you up in a hotel, and we will ask you a few questions on film. We won't embarrass you, I promise."

I continued to be reluctant to participate, asked the woman on the other end to hold for a second. Judy and I talked in hurried whispers, and we both decided it might not be a good decision. "I'm sorry," I said, "but I don't think I have much to offer. So, I'm going to have to say no to your offer at this time."

"Are you sure? We can't do the show without you," she said, trying to convince me to participate.

"I'm sorry, I just can't." The call ended. Judy and I talked about the topic of the show for most of the night.

Call number two came the next night, and it was Jerry.

"Hi, Steve, Jerry Dennis. Got a minute to talk?" Jerry was cheerful and upbeat.

"Sure. What's going on?" I asked, but I already knew he was calling about the show.

"You got a call from *Unsolved Mysteries* yesterday, right?"

"Yes, but I said I did not know what I had to offer and decided against the idea."

"Why?" Jerry wanted to know.

"Simple. I don't know what I would have to offer. We haven't talked in more than ten years, and I've forgotten most of it." Then, after a beat, "Jerry, I would love to help, but I just don't know what I would have to offer."

"Don't worry. I've got notes from the last time we visited. I can refresh your memory, no problem."

Jerry and I talked for most of an hour. He shared how he was watching *Unsolved Mysteries,* thought it might help his case with Mark, and gave them a call.

"I'm sure they thought I was some cook sitting around the TV with my buddies, drinking beer, and gave them a call. But when I explained I wanted to involve you, and you lived in Texas, they began to think there might be something to the idea."

"OK," I said. "Have the producer give me another call, and I will agree to help you with the show."

The next day, *Unsolved Mysteries* called back. This time I agreed to participate in the episode. We talked for several minutes, and they had a few questions to ensure I was fully committed to the show.

"We need you here next Friday. We'll overnight your ticket. Can you get to DFW?"

"Not a problem," I reassured them. DFW is a hundred miles north of where I lived. We checked, and using a local van service; I could get to and from DFW without a problem. Waco does have an airport with service to and from DFW, but the van was less than half the cost of flying.

"Good. We'll have a producer meet you at the airport in D.C. and take you to your hotel and get you settled. It would be best if you arrived in time to have dinner with everyone. All of this is on us. Other than getting to and from DFW, you will have no expenses. Any questions?"

After a few more pleasantries, the producer hung up, and I was scheduled to appear on *Unsolved Mysteries.* I called Jerry and told him that everything was set, and I would see him in D.C. the following Friday.

Part III

A young woman and a man met me when I arrived at Ronald Regan on Friday evening. They were holding up a sign with my name on it, and I went over and introduced myself. The man asked me to identify my bags. I told him I only had one, pointed it out, and he picked it up and put it in the car. The man drove with the woman in the front passenger sheet. We talked over the seats about Texas, my family, how I knew Mark, and similar small-talk topics.

They walked me to the front desk. The woman explained there was a reservation in my name, showed me some paperwork, and the desk clerk handed me a key.

"Check-in, take your bag to your room and come back down. We are all going to dinner tonight and talk about what will be happening over the next two days."

I did what they told me, and ten minutes later, I was back in the lobby. We walked the two blocks to the fanciest restaurant I had ever visited. I learned this was not going to be a Denny's type of dinner. There was a large table waiting for us, and after everyone took their seats, the woman made brief introductions. I was seated next to Jerry, and we had an opportunity to get reacquainted.

"Tomorrow morning," talking to Jerry and me, "you have off. We will be meeting with some government officials to go over the questions you," pointing to Jerry, "wanted to be answered. You are on your own for lunch, and I will pick you two up in the hotel lobby at 1:30."

We both nodded, indicating we understood.

"We have a short afternoon shoot for the two of you. We'll have an early dinner, and then we'll film the two of you this evening. Sunday, we'll film Jerry in and around D.C., and you'll be on your way back to your homes by five. Any questions?"

Replying in unison, Jerry and I said, "No."

"Good. Enjoy this wonderful food this evening, and we'll pick you up at your hotel tomorrow after lunch."

We were able to order individually. On a tight budget at home, I ordered the least expensive item I could find. A chicken dish for $15.00! It was good, but Jerry's $35 steak looked a lot better. Judy and I were struggling a little financially, and I was unprepared for the extravagance displayed at the restaurant.

Everyone introduced themselves and gave a brief bio on what they did 'back home' and their duties on this shoot. Jerry filled the rest of the meal with tales of paranoia, conspiracies, and problems other POW families encountered. Jerry told of one wife, hearing so many horror stories, decided to exhume her husband's body to ensure it was him. She was confident there would be no problems since dental charts identified him. So imagine her surprise when she opened the casket to find a fully dressed Naval officer laid out – but without ahead! Others found everything from empty caskets with sandbags to sandbags and body parts – a hand or afoot. The point Jerry was making was Mark's case was not as unique as one might think.

Most everyone finished the meal with an after-meal cocktail. However, I was not much of a drinker, with a glass of inexpensive champagne at New Year's being the limit of my alcohol consumption, so I decided to refill my diet coke.

The day had been a full one for me, and I was getting a little sleepy. However, back at the hotel, Jerry insisted I come to his room. He brought out a four-inch blue-cloth binder overflowing with papers in page protectors. He explained this was all the information he had collected over the years and highlighted several pages.

"Great. We have time tomorrow, and you can give me a more detailed look at what you've got."

"Here," he said, handing me the binder. "This is your copy. My way of saying thanks for being here. It means a lot to my family and me."

I took the binder and retreated to my room. I did not get much sleep that night as I spent much of it pouring over the pages. I think I fell asleep somewhere between 2 and 3 in the morning. It would be decades before I realized the significance of what Jerry gave me.

I was restless and told Jerry I was going to walk around the neighborhood and left the hotel. I walked up a couple of blocks, over a block and back down two blocks beyond the hotel, and back over and up to the hotel. We were in embassy territory, and several buildings had foreign flags flying in front of them. Jerry was in the hotel's restaurant when I returned. I joined him for a quick burger before the afternoon filming. After reviewing what he gave me the night before, I had a few questions, and he did his best to answer them.

The producers met us in the lobby, and we rode with them to a suburb of D. C. The tree-lined street showcased older homes, each expertly manicured. The producer told us the house owner was a friend of the director and had won an Academy Award, an Oscar, the previous year for a documentary. We saw the trophy, but the owner of the house was never on set. Instead, he was out of town on another documentary shoot.

The scene called for the two of us, Jerry and me, to talk while walking down the sidewalk. Just out of sight of the camera was the sound team. There was one tall gentleman with a large boom mike over our head and another man recording everything on a tape recorder. The scene required two shots. It was during the second shoot Jerry told me about the body's condition and the belief it had been blown apart by a case of grenades.

"There was shrapnel, a lot of shrapnel in almost every part of his body. There were also bits of wood and cellulose."

"Cellulose?" I asked.

"Paper. The kind of paper only used for the packing of hand grenades at the factory."

This fact caught me by surprise. More than a decade earlier, I had seen a tooth from the head of the remains, but Jerry never mentioned the actual condition of the body. I am sure the information was in the bonder Jerry gave me the night before, but it was just too much for me to comprehend at one time.

We had burgers on the patio at the back of the house. Jerry seemed cool as a cucumber, but I was figuratively bouncing off the walls. I was at an Oscar winner's home, about to film my interview, and worried about the questions they might ask.

After the meal, we moved inside, where they set up cameras for our interviews. I watched part of Jerry's interview but spent a lot of time on the patio with the second assistant cameraman. I can't give specifics now, but I learned they used different film types for various effects. I also learned the 2nd assistant cameraman loaded the film, which lasted ten minutes, and the 1st assistant exchanged the film in the camera. He also was responsible for positioning the camera. The cinematographer was the only one able to look through the camera, adjust the focus and film.

I also learned directors who were not union cinematographers could not look through the lens of the camera. That is why many had a camera lens dangling around their neck.

I learned Jerry was a talker, and after answering the question, the director asked Jerry to repeat his response more concisely.

"We just need the Reader's Digest answer," the director would say when Jerry finished his complete response.

They had allotted three hours for Jerry's interview and an hour for me. Starting at 7:30, they hoped to be done and gone before midnight. Instead, they finished Jerry's interview a little after one in the morning with just one more can of film left.

"We're sorry, Mr. Wilcox, but we can't film your interview tonight, and tomorrow we are on a tight schedule. So again, I am sorry you made the trip from Texas for no reason. We'll be in touch to reschedule your interview."

"No problem," I said. I was just excited to be on a set of a television show.

Jerry's congressman joined us for Sunday's shoot. He would be in the second scene, and we talked while walking to the Department of Justice building. Jerry explained the problem with Mark's enlistment physical.

"Well, if it was wrong, why didn't he correct it?" the congressman asked.

"You weren't in the military, were you?" I asked.

"No. I did not have that privilege."

"Well, sir, unless your job requires you to work in an area where you have access to these records, you never see them. Instead, they are given to you in a sealed envelope with your orders taped to the outside. Then, when you report to the new duty station, you hand everything over, and someone takes you to where you will be working."

"So, Mark never saw them?" he asked.

"Right. Mark never corrected the information because he did not know it was wrong. Even knowing it is wrong does not mean the Navy will correct it.

"What do you mean?" he wanted to know.

"Onboard ship, I had access to my records. Mine shows that I have a vaccination scar on my upper left arm because of the smallpox vaccination."

"Yeah, I have one."

"Well, I don't." I rolled up my sleeve and showed him. "I was re-vaccinated and still no scar. The Navy's answer? I have an invisible scar!"

"You're kidding," he said with a smile, believing I was teasing.

"No, sir. According to my Navy medical records, I have an invisible vaccination scar on my upper left arm."

He just shook his head in quiet disbelief.

We had to be quiet as they filmed Jerry coming down the sidewalk and up the stairs. They had to film it three or four times. The next scene was Jerry and the congressman shaking hands on the steps.

With those two scenes done, we finished filming in D.C. We rode in silence back to the hotel, where we grabbed our bags and rode to Ronald Regan for our flights home. Jerry and I talked for a few more minutes, and then it was time for him to board his flight back to

Florida, where he was now living. I hung around the airport for three hours until they announced my flight back to Dallas.

Back home, Judy wanted to know how it went, and the kids were excited to know what it was like on the movie set and when I would be on television.

"Did you meet Robert Stack?" my son was asking.

"No," I said. "He does all his filming one day a week back in Hollywood.

"Bummer," my son said.

Things returned to normal the next day when the kids were glued to the tv and Judy and I went back to work.

Part IV

It was apparent the producers of *Unsolved Mysteries* were not familiar with the Texas landscape.

"We are filming an episode in Amarillo. We can film your interview, say between 10 and 11 in the morning. You can drive in, do the interview and be home that night."

I hesitated.

"OK, Next month, we are in Midland if that is better for you."

"Neither one works for me. Both locations require a minimum of six hours on the road. Midland is probably closer to an eight-hour drive. Both will require an overnight stay."

It was their turn to hesitate.

"We will be filming the last part of your episode in California in three weeks. We'll be in El Segundo on Friday. We'll film your interview there. Then, the next day we are out near Victorville filming the Vietnam scene. I might have enough in the budget to cover your flight, but that's all. I don't have the budget to put you up in a hotel."

"Not a problem. My parents live in West Covina, and I can stay with them. I would like for my parents to be able to watch the filming on Saturday."

"I think we can arrange that. I will overnight your ticket tomorrow."

The company picked me up at LAX and drove me to the house for the filming.

"What's going on up there?" I asked as we passed a street blocked off with lots of trucks visible about halfway up the block.

"Tom Selleck is filming a scene from his new movie."

Between takes, they ushered me to the backyard. The producers laid out a catered meal, and Jerry and I watched the action from lawn chairs in the back.

There was a commotion at the front of the driveway. Jerry said, "One of the actors hit his head on the car door and had to go to the hospital. I guess he is back now." The car was a 59 Ford convertible, and the wing window had a sharp edge. He arrived back to set just as the producer called me for my interview.

The cameraman was seated on the arm of a couch, and the director was sitting next to him. They placed me inches from the camera and sat, leaning back in the chair to prevent breaking my nose on the camera. Halfway through the interview, the producer got up and told everyone to stop walking along the driveway. Their shadows showed up on the wall behind me. My answers were much shorter than Jerry's, and I apologized for the brevity of my responses. They said I was perfect, and my brief answers made it easier for them to edit the episode.

After dinner, we headed to an old Disney backlot for the scene where I talk to the Marine, telling me about his time with Mark. But unfortunately, I was about to become a royal pain in the butt!

"Wait, why am I in a Marine uniform? I was in the Navy."

"You both were at a Marine base, right?" The continued, "And Mark served with the Marines, didn't he?"

"Yeah, but I was stationed at the hospital in a Navy uniform."

After a half-hour delay, we back rolling.

"You can't have them walking and talking while lowering the colors. That is a court-martial offense," I explained.

They started with the flag at half-mast and began filming. The two actors stood at attention and saluted until they completed the lowering of the flag. Then they filmed the scene from four different angles.

True to their word, they drove me home and gave me three passes for the shoot the next day.

Before leaving, the driver said, "Be early, or you won't get in." Then the van pulled out of the driveway.

It was late in the evening, but my parents and I stayed up talking about the show, Judy, and their grandkids. Then we were up and on the way at the crack of dawn. At the entrance to the set, my dad handed the guard the passes, and we waved us through.

We were where they filmed the television show *China Beach*, a war drama about nurses in Vietnam. We watched a lot of the action from the building serving as the hospital on the show. It was also where they put the food for the cast and crew.

During the helicopter scene, a truck drove by as the helicopter came in with a casualty. The truck had a canvass cover on the back that kept blowing off during the scene. Finally, someone managed to tie the canvass down sufficiently to survive the helicopter's downdraft after the tenth time.

It was a fun day, and my parents were as excited as I was to watch the filming. My brothers and their families came over for a casual supper, and we had an enjoyable visit.

Mom made breakfast Sunday morning, and then we headed to LAX. My return trip left Los Angeles at noon and touched down at DFW just after 5 in the afternoon.

Part IV

I received a call from the producers with the episode's airdate. I managed to get myself on the local NBC affiliate's evening news as a teaser for the show that night. It was a good show. It was both entertaining and informative and provided zero information that would prove helpful. I helped Jerry weed through the 400 calls the show received that night. The most, by far, any show had produced thus far. I found one alleged former POW who knew of a POW with the nickname "preacher," however it was a bust: wrong place, wrong time.

What surprised me was the lack of Marines at Quang Tri and who might have participated in the ill-fated Operation Hastings. I thought maybe some of the Marines on helicopters returning to base might call. But, instead, 20% of the calls were about my teaser on the local NBC affiliate the night of the broadcast. Two weeks later, we had combed through all of the calls that sounded promising, producing no viable leads.

Within six months, Jerry and I lost contact. However, Mark's fiancée, Linda, was still in close contact with my wife, Judy, and we would learn bits and pieces about Mark through her.

I am sure Linda told Judy of Jerry's passing in 2002. However, through Linda, I learned of Bryan's efforts to raise money for private DNA testing and the results. The money was raised through a Facebook ® page, "Friends and Family of Mark V. Dennis." It was this group that made DNA testing possible.

Courtesy of the Dennis Family

THE MOST GENTLE OF ALL MEN

Mark was my first fiancée We met at church after he had joined the navy and when he was in corpsmen naval school. I was in nursing school. He planned to be a doctor when he came home. The last time I saw him was in February 1966 when we left him at Camp LeJeune. I've never met anyone like him, so giving and kind, so much strength in his faith in God. We were told he was shot down in a helicopter on July 15, 1966. 3 and 1/2 weeks later we buried a sealed casket. In November 1970 an issue of Newsweek carried a photograph of an "unknown POW" that his family thought was him. That, combined with an earlier report from the Navy that "a couple of men could have gotten out of the helicopter" sparked Mark's brother, Jerry, to begin a search for him. The body has been exhumed and examined, showing it to be a shorter man of Asian background with dental caries Mark never had. Also lead fuel in the bones from a jeep, not a helicopter. The matter was never settled to ease his parents' hearts before they died. In Miamisburg in the library park, the Stone to the Vietnam Vets lists him as MIA, not KIA. All who knew him here in his hometown, Miamisburg, Oh. will never forget him. Nor will I ever stop loving him - he truly gave all, in many ways we will never know.

Linda Mullins Williams

CHAPTER 8
The Exhumation

According to Greek Mythology, Zeus created a woman named Pandora and molded her after the goddess Aphrodite. He made her curious as well. Zeus brought her to Earth to be Epimetheus's wife and gave her a box as a wedding present. Pandora was instructed never to open that box, but she opened it since she was created to be curious. When Pandora did, she unleashed all of the evil that has since plagued the Earth. She closed it as quickly as she could, leaving only hope left inside the box.

Today, Pandora's box means anything that is best left undisturbed for fear of what might come out of it.

When Mark's family buried him in August 1966, the funeral included full military honors, and an honor guard escorted the body home. Jerry told me the Navy recommended the family not view the remains, and he placed a significant amount of importance on this statement. I thought Jerry overly dramatic at the time since one of my tasks at Lejeune was to teletype death notices. I typed several of these messages for active-duty personnel who died. It did not matter their age or manner of death, be it from disease or accident. Each of these notices contained the line, *recommend remains not to be viewed.*

The statement was not usual because it was an order given to the honor guard accompanying the body home. His duty was to prevent the family from opening the casket and viewing its content. Jerry said the honor guard's orders included sitting on the casket, if necessary, to prevent the casket from being opened. The government would handle the situation differently today. If the family was not allowed to view the remains, the casket would be sealed or glued shut.

Raising a casket from its earthly home is a complicated and costly procedure. Although Mark rested in the family plot, Jerry could not walk up to the cemetery custodians and say, "I want to dig up my brother's casket," and have it done. Today, a veteran's exhumation must have the approval of and be done with the supervision of the military. This procedure is in addition to whatever local and state forms may be required. The rules in 1966 were more relaxed than they are today. Jerry's notes contain confirmation the military authorized the exhumation of the body. Along with the notation that Jerry had managed to accomplish the exhumation on his own.

According to the legend, hope was the only emotion left in the box when Pandora shut it. When Jerry and the family elected to open the casket, they also abandoned hope. If the resident of that casket were their son and brother, then they would have to go through the grieving process all over again. But what if the body is not Mark, then what? Perhaps they were clinging to the hope the identification of that POW was wrong, and Mark might be alive. Whatever sliver of hope was present, that hope was replaced with frustration and anger—the family's frustration with the government's inability to see what everyone else saw. The body in that casket was not Mark. Frustration gave way to anger with lack of honor and respect shown to HM3 Mark Dennis through the family's lack of respect.

Whether he knew it or not, Jerry opened his own Pandora's Box, and it would take decades beyond his life before the box could be closed.

#

In August 1971, Jerry managed to have the casket exhumed and delivered to the Office of the Coroner of Montgomery County, Ohio. There, Chief Pathologist Dr. T. K. Baston, M.D. *opened the casket and made a limited examination of its contents.*

There was one curiosity in the casket. *An approximately 2-foot section of badly corroded and/or burned metal tubing.* When Jerry described this object to me, he identified it as not being from a helicopter or subjected to the elements. My questions were then and remain today twofold. First, where did this piece of pipe originate? Was it collected with the body, or did it come from someplace else? Second, why was the pipe included in the casket? It could not have been added to increase the weight as it would not have been a measurable additional weight. Was it placed in the casket to suggest the body was among the wreckage of a helicopter? Or was it a message from Central Identification Laboratory Hawaii that something isn't right with this body? I don't believe the Navy had a plausible rationale for its inclusion. They could have dismissed the pipe as Jerry did and concluded it should not have been there. If someone just threw the pipe in the casket to get rid of it, then what does it say about those charged with preparing bodies for shipping home.

USN identification tags bearing the name of Mark V. Dennis, with the USN SN, blood type, and, written out in full, Church of Christ. Dayton, Ohio, is home to Wright-Patterson Air Force Base. As such, it is not a stretch to believe Dr. Batson would be familiar with the information contained on the dog tags of service personnel. Rarely, if ever, is the denomination of the serviceman written out in full. I have not met a vet with tags containing their whole denomination spelled out, though one says he knew of one who did. Church of Christ is a mainstream protestant denomination, and Mark's dog tags should have read, "Prot." Writing the denomination out in full is an anomaly, and that the final "t" became the burr on the tag would have been sufficient reason to remake the tag. When Jerry opened the casket at the funeral home and grabbed the tags, the burr stuck into his thumb and drew blood.

Jerry concluded, "These tags have never been worn. They would have been too painful."

Other than the burr, what was on the tags did not interest Jerry. But then, Jerry was not in the military and would not have recognized the anomaly.

I said, "Jerry, the religious preference should be Prot. The full denomination is never mentioned in full because of the limited space on the tag. Looking at his records, they all say "Prot." Where did they get his full denomination?"

Jerry shrugged his shoulders and said, "I don't know." However, there was something else that bothered Jerry about the tag.

Continuing with his description of the tags, Dr. Batson noted, *The tags were smudged with a substance resembling smoke residue but were not distorted; the stamped information was perfectly legible.* Jerry was an arson investigator and recognized the problem right away. The tags were not involved in a helicopter crash and fire. The tags are thin, and an aircraft fire is super-hot. If the tags were in a helicopter crash and fire, there would necessarily be some distortion. However, as Dr. Batson specifically noted, there was no distortion of the print. Jerry would use his arson investigator resources and determined someone burned the tags with ordinary paper book matches. When asked, the Navy had no rationale for the burning of the tags.

As part of the televised interview, Navy spokesperson John Rodgers said, "It is an acceptable practice to manufacture new tags for a body when the identification has been made, but no tags were available." However, the Navy could not explain the burning of the tags. The inclusion of the pipe, the full denominational name, and the unexplained burning of the identification tags appear to be a lack of respect for the dead. When Jerry saw these at the funeral home, it is no wonder that he began to question whether there was a conspiracy or a cover-up in progress.

The report continues: *Badly charred human remains, skeletally intact except for absence of the distal forearms and hands, distal lower extremities and feet, mandible, and vault of the skull. The sternum and costal cartilages could not be identified.* Translated into layman's terms, the body was missing his lower jaw, upper right jaw, the roof of the mouth, arms at the elbow, and legs at the knee. Additionally, both the chest bone and ribs, if there, could not be seen. This observation could have been a treasure trove of information and evidence. Jerry would need to challenge the Navy's assertion this is the body of Mark Dennis. The importance of this evidence becomes apparent when reviewing the Certificate of Death prepared by the Navy.

The whole-body x-rays showed considerable bony detail, numerous metallic fragments scattered through the remnants of soft tissue, and one metallic fragment embedded in the region of the left maxillary sinus. The examination is not an autopsy, but the x-rays indicate this person was subjected to the explosion of one or more shrapnel grenades. The shrapnel is throughout the torso of the remains, and one is in the sinus cavity of the skull.

[Dr. Batson's] impression, based only on visual inspection of the remains and limited examination of the readily assessable bones, was that the remains were those of a male, short in stature, with a small skull. In 1963, when Mark was a tackle for the Miamisburg High School Viking football team, his height was listed as five-ten. Subsequent investigations, including one by the Naval Investigative Service, put Mark closer to six feet tall. Thus, regardless of Mark's hat size, which is unknown, it would be challenging to consider Mark to be of "short of stature." Dr. Brayton goes on to justify his conclusion.

Using this data, Dr. Bryaton made a rough estimate of stature using the method described by Krogman in The Human Skeleton in Forensic Medicine.

This method resulted in an estimated height of 69.5 cm. (66.7 inches), plus or minus 1.5 to 2.0 inches. Given Mark's high school height of 70 inches, this puts Mark beyond the body's margin for error. Based on everything known at the time, the maximum height of this body would have been 68.7 inches or more than an inch shorter than Mark's height in high school.

Dr. Batson provided a disclaimer that this was a visual inspection and *by no means adequate to justify a definitive conclusion*. However, it is also his opinion there was more than enough information to justify the study of the remains by experts in forensic anthropology.

The coroner's office repacked the casket and returned it to the funeral home. It was there, Jerry opened the casket himself and examined the contents. As he was preparing to unpin the tags that the burr dug into his thumb and drew blood. Stull, unaware of the significance of the coroner's report, Jerry removed the skull with the teeth.

It is impossible to say with any certainty what was going through Jerry's mind at the time. Hopefully, he had received and read the coroner's report before he opened the casket for himself. If this was true, Jerry and the family knew the remains in the casket were not his brother's. How solid of a plan Jerry developed at this time is another unknown. However, the family stood behind Jerry. And it was their new mission in life to return this body to the Navy and have their son and brother declared Missing in Action.

As an arson investigator, Jerry recognized the importance of physical evidence and removed the head. The two teeth were potential evidence proving the remains were not those of his brother. The body had no other recognizable features. Today, the skull would have been wrapped in a protective wrap, put in a bag, and then in a box. Unfortunately, the protective plastic wrap had not available in 1966. So the skull was most likely wrapped in paper and placed in a box.

After removing the skull, the family reburied the remains and added a ribbon to the headstone. "Here lies one known only to God." It would remain there for more than a decade before the family would exhume the body for a second time. Finally, the family decided the body would not be reburied. And the family plot would remain empty and eventually be sold back to the cemetery association.

With the second exhumation, there would be no involvement by the coroner's office. Instead, the remains would be placed in a box, and Mark's sister, Eileen, would put it in her car and drive it to the Forensic Anthropology Laboratory at Colorado State University. It would be there the expert examination recommended by Dr. Batson would take place.

Bryan said he did not know how his aunt managed the drive. However, she described the remains as "stinking to high heaven!"

In Jerry's narrative, he says medic John Lay, Mark's best friend from Vietnam, was in Fort Collins when the "casket" arrived. Bryan said his aunt drove the body to Fort Collins. From my conversations with funeral directors, before cremation, bodies are placed in various containers. So I assume Lay was referring to one of these paper caskets and not the large, ornate casket we usually visualize.

For the next three decades, the family would endure a hell on Earth. Jerry passed away in 2002 while undergoing open-heart surgery. Mark's sister, Anne, would lose a battle with cancer. The Navy would defy all logic and physical evidence, insisting the remains were those of Mark. The government did not return the skeleton. Instead, the returned cremated remains with a DNA sample the family may use for comparison. The government offered the laboratory services of a nearby Air Force Base.

I met Elsie Johnson, Mark's ex-sister-in-law, in 2021. She confirmed she witnessed one of the casket openings and observed a few bones were present. We talked about the ordeal and the cremation and burial. Elsie took a deep breath and said, "If it wasn't Mark's bones buried, it was still family. The unknown bones had been with the family for more than 50 years, and that made them family!"

With this funeral, Pandora's box began to close.

Courtesy of the Dennis Family

MARK "VESUVIUS" DENNIS (SPARKY)

Mark Dennis chose to join the United States Navy. They decided to send him to Vietnam. He served his country with pride and dignity. In July, 1966, the USN declared Mark as "Killed In Action", and shortly thereafter they shipped back to Miamisburg the body that they claimed was his. In 1970 that body was exhumed and was absolutely declared to not be Mark Dennis.

I was a 15 year old girl in 1966, and Mark was a good friend and engaged to one of my friends from our church. My world was devastated that day. OUR worlds were forever changed, not by Mark's death, but by the fact that there was no proof of his death and no body for us to lay to rest in Miamisburg, his home. I went to the traveling Vietnam Veterans' Wall. I, like so many others, made a paper copy of his name. That's all we have of Mark Dennis, his name. He was an exceptional human being who was a little shy before he got to know you, but a stand-up guy, and a wonderful friend. His potential was beyond amazing! I pray that he did survive and is healing people both physically and spiritually somewhere in the world. I won't write RIP for Mark, instead, I say God bless you, Mark, until we meet again.

DEBBY CURTNER-DUNHAM

CHAPTER 9
Meeting Alexander

The mangled and badly burned human remains discovered inside the casket intended for Mark was, at one time, a living, breathing human being. Therefore, I cannot simply refer to him as the remains, the body, or the corpse. Bryan Curtis, Mark's nephew, the new family spokesman after Jerry Dennis' death in 2002, said the family had a code name for the body. However, he also said he could not recall what it was.

Judith Viorst wrote a children's book titled *Alexander and His Terrible, Horrible, No Good, Very Bad Day.* I think anyone who has their body ripped apart by grenade explosions and subsequently burned beyond recognition indeed had a terrible, horrible, no good, very bad day. As a result, I have begun calling the contents of that casket Alexander.

We know very few facts about Alexander. There is a list of eighteen names on the Wall of Names for Lt. Cullers, who was the chopper's crew chief. Fifteen are from the helicopter crash. Three others are identified as ground force casualties. Over the years, through various means, we have determined Alexander was in his mid-twenties and of African descent. None of the losses fit the profile of Alexander. One was a Native American, one was Caucasian, and the only African American was only eighteen.

We know nothing about Alexander's personal life, his family life, or his education. We don't even know his name. He was in the military, but was he in the Army or the Marines? Was he an enlisted man or an officer? The odds favor him being an enlisted man, but was he drafted, or did he volunteer? What was his rank and Military Occupation Specialty? Was he married, single? Did he have a girl back home, was he engaged, or was he on his own? We know he died in Vietnam, but when, where, and how remains a mystery. If he died at Quang Tri, it was not on the day of the helicopter crash. It is doubtful we will ever know more than what we now know. Alexander has spent more than 50 years with the Dennis family as an unidentified corpse.

It is not a fair statement to say we know nothing about Alexander or how he died. However, thanks to the efforts of Dr. Michael Charney at the Forensic Anthropology Laboratory at Colorado State University, we know quite a bit. From CSU, we know that Alexander was most likely 67 ¼" and approximately 24 years old. In reading several abstracts dealing with anthropological estimates, the "most likely" designation means half of the population with the measurements used to determine these factors fit this norm. Therefore, 25% of the people with these measurements will be taller/older or shorter/younger.

Alexander was in 1966, and DNA was not yet available. Based on what I have learned of Operation Hastings, Alexander was not killed on that day and may not have been at Quang Tri at all. In 2014, the Dennis family paid for a DNA analysis using the most advanced techniques of the day, and the remains were probably of West African descent but definitely not related to Mark Dennis or any member of his family.

It is improbable Alexander was involved in the helicopter crash on July 15, 1966, at Quang Tri Provence. First, his injuries are inconsistent with the injuries of the twelve identified passengers killed in the crash. While there were no autopsies, it is logical to assume, based on what I have learned from those familiar with the Sea Knight, the passengers died from burns and/or smoke inhalation. This conclusion is based on the description of the accident by survivors Lucas and McLaine. The pilot stated the only grenades on board were the ones each marine carried. While the side gunner mentioned an explosion and spontaneous detonation of munitions and grenades, the condition of those recovered is inconsistent with his recollection.

Dr. Charney determined Alexander was near, carrying, or holding a case of grenades when they spontaneously detonated. This supposition was determined by the significant trauma sustained by Alexander and the amount of shrapnel and cellulose (paper) embedded in his remains. When, where, and why Alexander was near or had the grenades will never be known.

We also know that the body was burned. Alexander was most likely burned by regular leaded gasoline, given the significant lead in the skin. Tanks and large trucks used diesel fuel while aircraft used unleaded kerosene, known as JP3 or JP4. Jeeps and smaller vehicles used leaded gasoline – unleaded gasoline was not yet available.

There are multiple scenarios of how Alexander might have come to be in the condition he was in when the coroner opened the coffin. And while interesting, none of the scenarios tell us how Alexander wound up in a casket buried in Miamisburg, Ohio. And that is only one of many questions remaining unanswered.

Based on conversations with both marines and soldiers serving in Vietnam and elsewhere, the case of grenades being carried by Alexander exploded. Perhaps not the whole case, but several of them. There are various conjectures, but the consensus is that only two ways a grenade would detonate with the pin intact are concussion and heat. A tracer bullet penetrating the crate would possibly cause the grenade penetrated to explode. A regular round might have the same effect, but a tracer bullet produces more heat, and heat is one means of spontaneous detonation. If one grenade exploded, that concussion might set off additional grenades. However, heat is the most likely source of unintentional explosions. That is why grenades and munitions often spontaneously explode following an aircraft crash.

The question I needed answered is how, without the body being desecrated, could Alexander be burned as badly as he was and have the grenades unintentionally explode. The one scenario agreed to by several veterans involved cherry cans (small containers of fuel – gasoline and diesel), a supply truck, and a bullet. Although there was no smoking while unloading supplies, a few vets explained that some of those on the detail came with lit cigarettes in their mouths. If a cherry can had leaked fuel and the lit cigarette landed in the fuel on the ground, a fire and explosion could happen. Others attested that young soldiers did not handle their rifles properly. When putting the weapon aside to assist with the unloading, their rifles would go off and penetrate various items. If Alexander had the case of grenades in his hand and a bullet pierced a cherry can of gasoline, that would provide the fire needed to cause the grenades to go off and explain the extensive burns Alexander sustained. I learned about two other scenarios. Friendly fire. A stray bullet from a soldier shooting at a target (enemy soldier) near the truck may have accidentally hit the truck's fuel tank or a cherry can. The last scenario involves an enemy sniper shooting the truck. Either of these scenarios might have produced the injuries noted and the burns the body sustained.

The veterans also agreed that a helicopter crash could produce enough heat for spontaneous explosions. I eventually discounted this supposition as a possibility since the pilot said no supplies were on board. Since the body had packaging paper embedded with the shrapnel in its body, a case of grenades had to be involved.

Quang Tri and Operation Hastings were not particularly friendly when it came to helicopters. LZ Crow was too small to handle the planned influx of Sea Knights. As a result, we lost several choppers. These losses caused the path leading to LZ Crow and pilots calling the pathway "Helicopter Alley." Given there are no reports of the helicopter exploding on or shortly after impacting the ground, it is improbable the injuries sustained by Alexander were from the crash itself. There were twelve marines positively identified by dog tags and dental records. None of their death certificates reflect any trauma resembling those of Alexander.

I was sharing some of this information with another veteran. I said, "Either the body the family received was switched in transit, or the doctor completing the form phoned it in." a "phoned in" report means the examination was not done, or at least, not done in person. Did the doctor write down what might be expected of a helicopter crash? "Completely burned" as a description of the body and "burned" as the rationale for no fingerprints.

"Anything is possible. It was total chaos over there at times," he reminded me.

The doctor signing Mark's certificate of death also signed at least one other from the crash. Since this corpse was not completely burned, identification was able to be made by comparing dental charts. This procedure tells me the doctor is not just "phoning in" his reports. Therefore, the only conclusion is that they switched bodies between his examination and arrival in Miamisburg, Ohio.

*Courtesy of the Dennis
Family*

MARK V DENNIS AND HIS NOBLE FAMILY:
VICTIMS OF WAR AND OF BAD MEDIA

The Mark V. Dennis case is a heartbreaking example of the sacrifices of war and the devastating impact to family. The case is potentially an example of misidentification of remains during the confusion of war, and certainly a case of sloppy reporting involving a photo of an "unidentified" POW, once believed by the Dennis family to be Mark, that was published in Newsweek magazine in 1970. Life Magazine had identified the POW as Lt. Paul E. Galanti in 1967. These elements would tragically combine to send Mark's family through a heartbreaking search for the truth over the following 50 years.

The Mark V. Dennis case forces us to wonder how many American families may have buried misidentified remains from the Vietnam War and should be a lesson to journalists about the importance of fact-checking rather than going with an assumption.

Such is the cruelty of war. Such is the sacrifice of HM3 Mark V. Dennis and his patriotic family.

Veteran 2000

CHAPTER 10
Where's Mark?

After reading all the reports and statistics and looking at the test results, I have just one question. Where is Mark? I am not trying to be facetious or a smart-ass. It is a simple question I assumed no one had thought to ask over the past fifty-plus years. The body everyone has been fighting over is not the one Lieutenant Commander Samuel Lugo, M.D., MC, USNR, examined on July 25, 1966. A First Lieutenant then approved this report of the United States Marine Corps, whose signature is illegible.

During the filming of *Unsolved Mysteries*, Jerry said all of the bodies were burned beyond recognition. I protested because several had notations of scars and tattoos while dental charts identified others. Jerry dismissed the information saying, "They copied the information from their medical records." Had I been able to persuade Jerry to take a closer look at the death certificate, we might have been successful in returning the remains given to the Dennis family and having Mark classified as MIA.

The government is not free of complicity in this boondoggle. One of the strongest arguments the body was that of HM3 Dennis would have been the death certificate. Either they did not look at the NAVMED-N, Certificate of Death prepared by Dr. Lugo, or they did look at the death certificate and did not care about the certificate, and the body did not match.

Even the part of the death certificate transcribed from the medical records the government could not get right. According to Mark's medical records, his eyes were brown, yet it says the eyes are blue on the death certificate. We know eyes do not change color upon death. So, either the clerk typing the data from the medical records once again made an error, or the corpse's eyes were blue. If it is a clerical error, those completing these forms point to the lack of concentration and attention to detail. If the eyes were, in fact, blue, then the body does not match the medical records of Mark Dennis and must be declared not to be that of the missing medic.

Box 21 asks for "Marks and Scars."

Dr. Lugo's Description: *Completely Burned*

Dr. Batson's description: *Badly charred human remains, skeletal intact except for absence of the distal forearm and hands, distal lower extremities and feet, mandible, and vault of the skull. The sternum and costal cartilages were not identified.*

Both are, in theory, a visual examination of the remains of Mark Dennis. However, they are so significantly different that it would be difficult to conclude anything else other than the body Dr. Lugo described is not the body Dr. Batson's described. In other words, they had switched the body.

Box 21: Fingerprints

Dr. Lugo's description. *Burned*

Dr. Batson's description: *...the absence of the distal forearm and hands.*

Dr. Lugo is reporting it is impossible to obtain fingerprints due to the burned condition of the body. However, Dr. Batson says fingerprints are possible because the body has no hands.

Box 27 (a) "DISEASE OR CONDITION DIRECTLY LEADING TO DEATH."

Dr. Lugo's description: *Completely Burned*

I am not a doctor, but it would seem to me when a set of remains on your table missing both feet, both ankles, both lower legs, both hands, both wrists, both forearms, their chest bone, ribs, and three-fourths of the mouth would be a more significant cause of death, even though the body was burned.

Giving Dr. Lugo the benefit of the doubt, that the burning of the body preceded the explosion resulting in visible trauma, the trauma indeed would have been considered significant enough for Dr. Lugo to mention it elsewhere.

Box 27(b) "ANTECEDENT CAUSE"

Dr. Lugo's description: *None*

None? Really? Is a Lieutenant Commander, a medical doctor in the United States Navy, so inept and so blind that he would not consider that missing one's chest, arms, legs, and mouth not contributing to the death of HM3 Dennis?

BOX 27 (c) "OTHER SIGNIFICANT CONDITIONS CONTRIBUTING TO THE DEATH BUT NOT RELATED TO THE DISEASE OR CONDITION CAUSING DEATH."

Dr. Lugo's description: *The box is left blank*

Again, is it fair to assume the trauma experienced by the United States Armed forces member was not a significant condition contributing to his death? If what Dr. Batson described cannot be considered a primary, antecedent, or significant condition, how would Dr. Lugo and the Navy classify the body's condition?

BOX 30 "SUMMARY OF FACTS RELATED TO DEATH"

Dr. Lugo explains Mark Dennis was (a) a passenger on a helicopter shot down by enemy ground fire, (b) Dennis was one of thirteen casualties, and (c) he was originally identified by a process of elimination.

After being hit, the Sea Knight dropped to no more than 40' above the ground, and stalling and crashing from that height would not generate the injuries sustained by this corpse. Additionally, none of the other dozen fatalities sustained any injuries similar to those experienced by this alleged passenger.

There are four possibilities for the discrepancies noted by the two medical examiners.

1. There is a cover-up at the highest level. A flag officer, a general, or an admiral, for whatever reason, determined Mark Dennis was not going to be an unaccounted-for casualty. But why? Mark was a remarkable young man, especially to his family. But he was not of a notable family, nor was he a member of the intelligence community. He was a hospital corpsman and acting chaplain for his unit. There is nothing in his background or service record that would justify the falsification of his record to this magnitude.

2. Lugo did not examine the body. I have had both Vietnam and middle east vets tell me shortcuts happened because of the chaos of the time. This type of report is often referred to as a phoned in review. He is given the form and fills it in with the most likely answers. Mark was on a helicopter the crashed and burned. Therefore, the body was completely burned, and fingerprints were not possible because of the burns.

3. The third, and most likely scenario, is they switched the body. It might have been accidental as the information attached to the body bags would sometimes come off. Someone picked up the slips that had fallen off and accidentally placed them on the wrong bag. This switch could have happened in Phu Bi, where the bodies were before being sent to the mortuary at Da Nang. It could have happened at the Central Identification Laboratory – Hawaii, where the final processing for flying home occurred.

4. The original body examined by Dr. Lugo, who know it was not Mark, may have been identified as another Marine after Dr. Lugo's examination. The Navy had already notified the family of Mark's death and that his body was being shipped home. However, the body witched with the body Dr. Lugo examined had not yet had a NAVMED-N completed. This oversight may be why the honor guard had orders not to allow the family to view the remains.

However it happened, wherever it happened, the one thing is obvious. The body described on Mark Dennis's NAVMED-N is not the body given to the family.

Courtesy of the Dennis Family

THANK YOU

Thank you for your service as a Hospital Corpsman 3rd Class with the 1st Marine Division. Semper Fi. Thank you for the lives you saved. Monday was the 43rd anniversary of the Fall of Saigon. It has been too long, and it's about time for us all to acknowledge the sacrifices of those like you who answered our nation's call. Please watch over America, it stills needs your strength, courage and faithfulness. Rest in peace with the angels.

Lucy Micik

CHAPTER 11
Presenting Jerry's Case

In February 2017, Eileen Brady had the bones she received from Defense POW/MIA Accountability Agency cremated and buried with her parents. When asked if she believed the bones were that of her brother, she replied, "It's personal." For more than three decades, until he died in 2002, Jerry Dennis led his family's fight to have his brother, Mark, be listed as Missing in Action rather than Killed in Action. Jerry amassed an arsenal of information that the government ignored, dismissed, or identified the conclusions as erroneous.

Jerry's plight was an informal fight with no independent arbitrator to determine the merits and quality of the evidence. It was an argument of letters and phone calls, and Jerry jumped the gun on a few issues. At first, Jerry went through the appropriate channels and sought permission. Finally, however, he grew impatient and managed to proceed before receiving approval from the government. Jerry told me the government tried to talk him out of doing the *Unsolved Mysteries* segment, but he did the piece anyway.

When we met to film *Unsolved Mysteries*, Jerry gave me a four-inch binder of information related to his brother's death. Some of the information he pressed and other information he concluded to be unimportant. I have added the suggestions and opinions I would offer to Jerry if we proceeded with his case today.

Identification Tags

The dog tags were smudged by smoke from a low-grade fire (Batson), possibly suggesting they had been in the helicopter crash. When asked, the government had no rationale for the altering of the tags.

Given limited space, a military personnel's religious preference is abbreviated. Mark's original identification tag would have had "Prot" for his religious preference. His specific denomination, CHURCH OF CHRIST, is spelled out in full on the newly created dog tags. That created a burr that would have made the tags too painful to wear.

Jerry brought the burning of the tags up during the filming of the "Missing Medic" episode. He did not bring up the denominational issue. The Navy did not have a response to the query. In the end, the tags are more of a curiosity than anything else. I would probably have suggested Jerry ignore them.

NAVMED-N #1

The NAVMED-N is the military death certificate. It is a visual inspection of the body, noting anything out of the ordinary, such as missing body parts. Based on the information on the form, we may assume that the remains were in a condition similar to the twelve identified passengers killed due to the same helicopter crash.

This omission is significant, and I do not know why Jerry did not proceed with this. Jerry told me the information was taken from the medical records and dismissed it. He was right, and he was wrong. The Navy copied biographical data on the front from the deceased's medical records. But even there is an error. The eye color is wrong.

More importantly, how can Jerry successfully challenge what isn't there. The Navy identified a body based on a process of elimination but then did not give the family the body. When the family first exhumed the body, the family had a reason to believe Mark may still be alive. How can Jerry, or anyone else, challenge the government's findings if they have misplaced the evidence?

NAVMED-N #2

In reality, this is the reverse of the above. There is a body but no NAVMED-N. We have a body without a death certificate. Additionally, the injuries are inconsistent with the injuries sustained by the twelve previously identified fatalities from this incident.

Jerry focused on the obvious; this was not Mark Dennis. Based on anthropological data, the body was too short and too old. And in theory, this should have worked. The Navy dismissed the age difference as insignificant (JD). Depending on the part of the torso used, there are multiple estimations of height. I am not able to ascertain how or if Jerry addressed the three major issues.

1. *From where did the body come? It is impossible to determine where this body originated, whether it was Army or Marine, when, where, and how or who killed him with no death certificate.*
2. *This person died from multiple grenade explosions. From where did the grenades come? According to the pilot (JD), there were no stores on board the craft. If there were no cases of grenades on board, where did they originate?*
3. *If grenades exploded due to heat from the helicopter fire following the crash, how come only this one body was affected? He was a medic. How come no other body experienced grenades exploding? No other bodies, especially those corpses subjected to the intense heat and fire, were burned beyond recognition but showed no evidence of being exposed to exploding grenades.*

How tall are you?

Jerry pinned all of his hopes on the size and age of the body received. For those who knew Mark know the remains are not his. Knowing the truth and proving it is not the same. Jerry had a large hill to climb, trying to confirm Mark's actual height.

As society has evolved, so has the safety precautions for sports. Today's youth participating in extra-curricular activities from football to band require an actual physical. This document gives an official record of height and weight. In 1966, Mark's height was measured in two ways. First, there might be tape on the wall like you see at your neighborhood convenience store. The athlete would stand against the tape, and they would record the heigh. Second, some schools had a scale with a device attached to measure height. Either way, these are considered anecdotal and not official measurements. Being healthy and athletic, Mark did not have to have an official measurement of his height and weight.

The remains are partial, with no legs below the knees. Thus, they use a bone to determine the approximate height. Depending on the bone used, the approximate height may vary, as will the margin for error. Using the femur as the bone point of reference, the femur measurement in this illustration is 2.38 cm. Other calculations include gender and race. For this illustration, they used male and Caucasian.

2.38 X 45.3 = Height in cm +/- 3.27 cm

X 0.3937 = Height in inches +- 1.3 inches

Height estimation: 66.6" +/- 1.3 inches

The height range therefore is 65.3" – 67.9"

The military has eight estimated eights ranging from a short 64.3" to a tall of 70.9 inches. Six of the eight, however, are in the 65-to-68-inch range. This measurement is consistent with the three measurements the family has done. So what does all this mean? First, if the person you are trying to identify matches the "most likely" height, the odds are 1::2 you have a match. Second, moving out of the most likely range, either way, you now cut your odds in half to 1::4 or less.

What about Mark? How tall was he really? Mark's induction physical indicates his height as 67 14" on his induction physical and 69 ½" on another document. He is listed as 70" tall in his high school's football program, and using the second reading of 69 ½" puts Mark beyond six of the eight estimates from the government.

As mentioned before, there is not an official record of how tall Mark was, but there is ample anecdotal evidence putting Mark much closer to 72" than 67 ¼" shown on his physical,

And the taller Mark is shown elsewhere in his records.

The notes Jerry put together indicate a second unidentified document with a height closer to what Mark would have been at induction. I would have done everything I could to obtain a copy of that record as a basis for how tall Mark was at induction. This official government document puts Mark outside the margin for error of nine out of the eleven estimates arrived at by both family and military anthropologists.

Jerry told me, "CILHI doesn't believe Mark experienced a growth spurt while in the service."

"It's not so much about a growth spurt," I said, "as it is a loss of height. How does a growing boy shrink three inches in six months?"

RACE

There are only three races. To be politically correct, corpses are identified as African, Western European, and Pacific Islanders. Mark was a tall Western European young man of strong, athletic build. Dr. Batson described the unknown soldier as being of "slight built." Dr. Charney suggests he was of African descent. Dr. Maples did not come right out and say, "Dr. Charney, you're wrong." However, he did say, "I can't get the same degree of bow stated by Dr. Charney."

Although neither Dr. Maples nor Dr. Charney would say conclusively, the suggestion the body may be of a different race than Mark is significant. This suggestion should be exploited. The Navy cannot explain the burning of the dog tags, the entire denomination on the tags, the shrapnel in the body, most of the Navy's anthropologists put the remains considerably shorter than the height Mark was known to be at the time of his death, and everyone puts the body older than Mark was at the time of his death, so why can't they be wrong about the race as well. Nothing the government has said or done has discounted or destroyed the credibility of any of the evidence Jerry Dennis has amassed.

Courtesy of the Dennis Family

REMEMBERING AN AMERICAN HERO

As an American, I would like to thank you for your service and for your sacrifice made on behalf of our wonderful country. The youth of today could gain much by learning of heroes such as yourself, men and women whose courage and heart can never be questioned.

May God allow you to read this, and may He allow me to someday shake your hand when I get to Heaven to personally thank you. May he also allow my father to find you and shake your hand now to say thank you; for America, and for those who love you.

With respect, and the best salute a civilian can muster for you, Sir

Curt Carter

CHAPTER 12
Closing the Box

Mark was a tall, dark, handsome young man with his whole life in front of him. He was profoundly religious and cared deeply for his fellow man. Jerry always said Mark wanted to be a missionary while his fiancée, Linda, says Mark had his sights on becoming a pediatrician. Either way, it was clear he was not self-centered. Instead, he felt the calling to help his fellow human beings.

He enlisted in the Navy's Hospitalman Recruitment Program, which means after Bootcamp, he would be guaranteed immediate training as either a hospital corpsman or a dental technician. Mark chose the hospital corpsman route and served at three duty assignments. The first was aboard the aircraft carrier Wasp. From there, he went to the Naval Hospital, Camp Lejeune, North Carolina. While there, he transferred to the Marines and FMF duty. After FMF Training, Mark deployed to Vietnam, where on the evening of July 15, 1966, he was one of eighteen who gave their last full measure for his country.

Did he enlist in the Navy due to the brewing Vietnam War? Did he enlist because this might provide valuable training should he become a doctor? Or did he enlist, hoping the educational benefits might offset the cost of pre-med and medical school? Unfortunately, we may never know why he enlisted, only that he did.

Mark certainly shared with his family he volunteered for Vietnam. Whether he actually volunteered or made the statement to calm the fears his family expressed is another question we cannot answer. Those of us who had the privilege of knowing and working with Mark knew if the opportunity presented itself, he would have stepped up and added his name to the list. That is the Mark I remember and admire.

When Jerry brought me on board with the television episode, there was no shortage of conspiracy theories. There were several books on the horrors that was Vietnam. Many of the authors reported being accosted by men in dark suits and black SUVs. Some wrote of having themselves and their families threatened, having their phones tapped, and told explicitly to stop writing the book. But, of course, they did not stop, and they published their books. I even read a few. To the best of my knowledge, none of these threats became a reality. Jerry even believed his phone line was tapped and could give some convincing arguments.

While I do not have first-hand knowledge, this is not to say things happened that I would not wish on my worst enemy. They did. The United States Government sought to discredit Jerry and his family in their fight. Their fight for what? Their struggle for the truth is that the government has no inclination where Mark may be. The fight to have the government publicly acknowledge what they privately admitted. The body given to the family was not that of HM3 Mark V. Dennis.

Jerry was not wrong in his paranoia. He knew the government had lied about certain things, which begs the question about what else have they lied. When confronted with the overwhelming evidence their assumptions were wrong, they dug in even further. When they did DNA testing in the late 80s and early 90s, the tests came back as inconclusive. Coincidentally, the DNA testing was done when the Defense POW/MIA Accountability Agency secretly changed Mark's status from KIA to MIA. They even used science with a confidence rating below 75% to say with absolute certainty that the remains were Mark's. On television, the government reported all they recovered all remains from the helicopter crash. We know this was a lie since one passenger, Mark Dennis, was found under the excavated wreckage in 2014.

When I began to write Mark's story, I hoped I would find a way to bring closure to the family that our military establishment had denied for more than fifty years. Like Jerry, I was convinced there was a conspiracy involved. I was wrong. I attribute most of my questions to sloppy record-keeping than a deliberate attempt to deceive. Part of the ineptness may be attributed to the reality and chaos of war. But not even that can explain away everything. The most important questions cannot be answered because the decisions were irrational. With no evidence of Mark Dennis ever being on that helicopter, how can it be a rational decision to determine his death and then substitute a body in his place? The sensible explanation would be *Missing and Presumed Dead!* By replacing the body, Alexander, for Mark, another family has been from honoring their loved one. There is another family out there with questions regarding their son/brother/husband's whereabouts.

Why was it so essential to have Mark Dennis declared dead?

Why was it necessary to substitute a body known not to be his?

Why not admit the error?

Why not be honest with the findings?

These are the remaining questions we can never answer. Whoever made these decisions in 1966, 1990, 2014 are either deceased or anonymous. No one signed their name to the mandate. We are unable to go to their office, knock on their door and ask for answers. Even if we found them, what could they possibly say to the Dennis family that would justify forcing them to spend hundreds of thousands of dollars and put them through decades of mental anguish, pain, and suffering?

To paraphrase a comment John Rodgers made during the *Unsolved Mysteries* broadcast, **I believe in my heart of hearts Mark is now resting alongside his parents in Florida.** We know the government foundMark underneath the helicopter, and I think I know how he came to be there. I see how the number of fatalities has gone from 11 to 13 to the 15 it is today. Not because of any conspiracy but a lack of pride in the assigned task. Acting on partial information has given some the impression someone was trying to hide something.

Jerry, I have finished the job you unknowingly gave me. You would have found the answers, I am sure. Unfortunately, the good Lord had other plans. DNA, the internet, and a network of veterans have provided me with the tools not available to you. I did not get all of the answers to your questions, but I have, I hope, answered the crucial ones.

With that, I have shoved as many problems and concerns possible back into Pandora's Box, and I have glued, soldered, duct-taped and hammered it shut.

REST IN PEACE, CHARLES, VERA, JERRY, ANNE, ELAINE
AND
HM3 MARK V. DENNIS USN/FMF

*Courtesy of the Dennis
Family*

YOU ARE NOT FORGOTTEN

*The war may be forgotten but the warrior will always be remembered !!!!
All gave Some-Some gave All. Rest in peace Mark. :-(*

Jerry Sandwich

FINAL MISSION OF U.S. MARINE CORPS HELICOPTER CH-46A TAIL NUMBER 152500

Operation Hastings (15 July – 3 August 1966) began with a series of combat assaults by 2nd & 3rd Bns, 4th Marines. LZ CROW, about 10 km N-NW of Cam Lo, was barely large enough for 4 CH-46s. The first landings went OK, then one landed long in the trees, one was shot down, and two had a rotor disc collision in the LZ. A reaction force from 1st Plt, E Co, 2nd Bn, 1st Marines was sent in on CH-46A 152500 to protect the downed aircraft while the 3rd Bn, 4th Marines went about their affairs. The element aboard 152500 included infantrymen, Corpsmen, and engineers from A1st Eng Bn whose job it was to see about clearing the LZ. The HMM-265 history states that at 1815 on 15 July 1966, EP-171 was hit by heavy enemy 12.7 automatic weapons fire and subsequently crashed.

Both pilots and the gunner survived, with minor burns sustained by the pilots and second and third degree burns by the gunner. Both pilots performed in an outstanding manner while maneuvering the burning aircraft toward a landing site. The crew chief SGT Robert R. Telfer died despite the efforts of the gunner, SGT Lucius, to save him. The official USMC Vietnam History for 1966 contains a photo of this aircraft taken from LZ Crow by photographer Horst Faas (1933 – 2012), a German photo-journalist and two-time Pulitzer Prize winner best known for his compelling images of the Vietnam War. The photo clearly shows flames coming from the aft and smoke from the cockpit area while the CH-46 is still at least a 100 feet in the air.

On page 165 this history quotes COL Vale, the Infantry battalion CO on the ground at the time: The last helicopter (152500), carrying reinforcements from the 2d Bn, 1st Marines, came under ground fire from the ridge on the south side of the valley. The pilot tried to land in the LZ, but as he slowed down and hovered, the smoke got into the flight compartment, and he had to move forward to keep the smoke out. As a result, he overshot the LZ and after moving over the CP tried to set down again. By this time the helo was rolling and barely remaining airborne. The pilot had to move forward again and then crashed on the edge of the area in which the CP and 81 mortars were set up.

Thirteen men died and 3 others were injured in this event. PFC Michael A. Gooden was aboard the aircraft and died of burns received in the crash. He is miscoded in the CACCF as a ground casualty. CPL William J. Lilly and HN John N. Morris are the two men killed on the ground. They too are miscoded in the CACCF, but the other way around--as passengers. The names of the other passengers on 152500 include CPL Orson H. Case, HM3 Andrew P. Chamaj, CPL Paul R. Chambers, PFC James W. Cherrick, 2LT Ronald K. Cullers, PFC Michael A. Cunnion, HM3 Mark V. Dennis, CPL James M. Reid, PFC Carl W. Schloemer, SSGT Herolin T. Simmons, and PFC Gerald E. Stubstad. In addition to the 15 men killed in the crash (1 aircrew, 12 passengers, 2 on the ground), three other Marines died in the ground fighting (Parts of this report provided by Ken Davis) [Taken from vhpa.org; image from kichbu.multiply.com]

Note: I do not have the rights to the photograph mentioned in this narrative.

CORPSMAN UP!

*Courtesy of the Dennis
Family*

In withering fields of fire, through booby traps and mortar bom-
bardments,
even with the enemy in close hand-to-hand combat, when the call came
for "Corpsman Up!", you left the safety of your cover because one of
your Marines needed you.

It was your care that saved the life of that Marine. There were times
when you were not able to keep him with us. Even then, a hand held
and a soothing word from "Doc" helped to ease the passage of a dying
comrade.

Now we hold your hand and tell you that through all eternity,
Marines
will forever be inspired by your example of courage, devotion, and
honor.
We will remember you and hold a special place in our hearts for the
man called "Doc".

Rest in peace,
SEMPER FI

Graphics

Sea Knight Similar to this Chinook
(c) Getty Images, used with permission

This Army Chinook helicopter looks almost identical to the Navy and Marine's Sea Knight helicopter. Both were built by a division of Boeing aircraft. Mark was on a Sea Knight.

**Vietnam as it was
divided in 1966**
*(c) Getty Images, used
with permission*

Vietnam was divided approximately at the 17th parallel with a 4-6 mile wide buffer known as the DMZ or Demilitarized Zone. Quang Tri Provence is adjacent to the DMZ near the Laotian border.

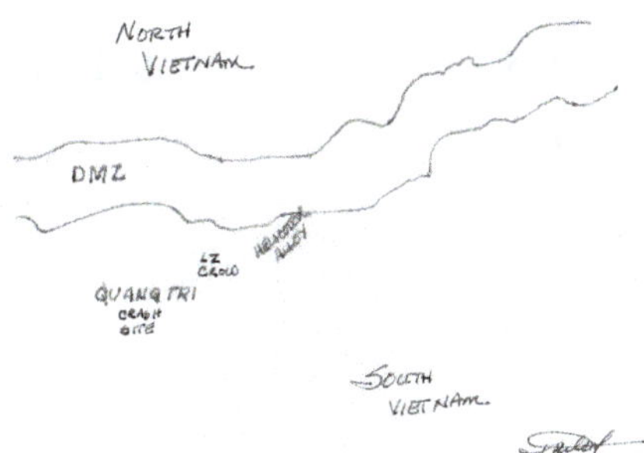

Hand-drawn map by the author

Rose 6 approached LZ Crow through what had become known as "Helicopter Alley," so named for the many helicopter crashes at the site. The position of both LZ Crow and the crash site are approximations.

Resources

Curtis, Bryan – Miscellaneous notes, oral commentary, unpublished correspondence, and graphics.

Defense POW/MIA Accountability Agency – https://www.MPAA.gov

Dennis, Jerry – Miscellaneous notes, oral commentary, unpublished correspondence, and graphics.

Erwin, Linda – Oral commentary

Johnson, Elsie – Oral commentary

Johnson, Neva B. (et al) - Defense Technical Information Center: - https://apps.dtic.mil/sti/pdfs/AD0699826.pdf

Kuehn, Carrie M. B.A. (et al) "Validation of Chest X-ray Comparisons for Unknown Decedent Identifier – National Library of Medicine - https://pubmed.ncbi.nlm.nih.gov/12136980/

National Library of Medicine - Abstract – Estimation, and Evidence in Forensic Anthropology - https://pubmed.ncbi.nlm.nih.gov/19226642/

Patidor, Kalpana (et al) - "Effects of High Temperature on Different Restorations in Forensic Identification:Dental Samples and Mandible" Journal of Forensic Science (online) https://www.ncbi.nlm.nih.gov/pmc/articles/PMC3009553

Sturkey, Marion F. – *Bonnie Sue: A Marine Corps Helicopter Squadron in Vietnam* – Heritage Press International (1996)

Validation of chest x-ray comparisons for Unknown Decedent Identification(www.astm.org/DIGITAL_LIBRARY/ JOURNALS/FORENSIC/ PAGES/JFS15450J.htm)

Wall of Faces (Mark V. Dennis) - https://www.vvmf.org/Wall-of-Faces/12964/MARK-V-DENNIS/

Williams, Linda Mullins – Oral Commentary

www.ingramcontent.com/pod-product-compliance
Lightning Source LLC
Chambersburg PA
CBHW061005050726
47592CB00003B/1355